THE POWER *of* PERCEPTION

The Power of Perception

How Your Inner Perspective Creates Your Outer Reality

Jeremy Yates

Published by Game Changer Publishing

Paperback ISBN: 979-8-90158-208-4
Hardcover ISBN: 979-8-90158-142-1
Digital ISBN: 979-8-90158-143-8

www.GameChangerPublishing.com

This book is dedicated to my wife and daughters,
who give me a new perspective on life every day,
and to anyone who is looking to learn something new.

ADVANCE PRAISE

"Jeremy Yates is an accomplished hospital-based educator who brings his wealth of experience and knowledge to the discussion of the science of perception. He offers an understanding of perception that can be effectively utilized to create a positive culture within any organization by clarifying how we individually perceive our environments. The Power of Perception *is essential reading for all work environments where the goal is to positively influence team communication for enhanced collaboration and better outcomes."*

Thomas Saggio, RN, MSN, MHS, PMH-BC
| Director of Behavioral Health Operations

"Jeremy Yates brings a rare blend of clinical expertise, leadership wisdom, and genuine compassion to The Power of Perception. *His perspective challenges readers to rethink how they interpret the world around them—and how those interpretations influence their actions. This book is insightful, empowering, and exactly the kind of work that elevates both professionals and communities."*

Stacey Lindley, MSN, RN, CCRN
| Patient Care Manager, Center for Practice Excellence

"Useful and engaging content for young adults and adults. A handbook to self-control of who we are in this world."

Louis Buck, RN

"Working alongside Jeremy Yates has been an inspiring experience. In The Power of Perception, *Jeremy thoughtfully explores how each of us views the world through our own lens and how we intentionally seek others' perspectives, which gives us the power to shape our choices, strengthen relationships, and expand our influence. Jeremy's passion for nursing education and his support of my journey to earn a doctoral degree reflect the same principles shared in this book—fostering growth, collaboration, and the ability to drive meaningful improvements in quality and outcomes within our organizations."*

M. Mika Walter, MSN, MBA, RN, NE-BC, FACHE

READ THIS FIRST

Just to say thanks for buying and reading my book, I would like to connect and offer you some free resources for your journey!

Scan the QR Code Here:

THE POWER *of* PERCEPTION

How Your Inner Perspective Creates Your Outer Reality

JEREMY YATES

FOREWORD

The year is 2005. I am the executive director of Project Helping Hands, an organization that deploys medical teams worldwide to provide care in underserved and underdeveloped regions. At that time, I was personally leading a medical team into the jungles of Bolivia, and among the volunteers on that mission was a young nursing student named Jeremy Yates.

Fast forward 20 years, and I receive a telephone call from Jeremy, who is now not only a registered nurse but also a doctor of nursing. During those two decades, he has served as a critical care nurse, firefighter, nursing educator, and nurse administrator, earning the respect of colleagues throughout the nursing profession. Jeremy was calling to seek my advice about authoring his first book.

Now I have been given the privilege not only of previewing Jeremy's work but also of writing this foreword. As I read through this book, I found myself with one small regret: that I did not have a resource like this during my own professional journey. Jeremy does an excellent job of presenting important concepts that help us better understand who we are as individuals and how that understanding can shape us into stronger, more effective leaders.

Drawing from more than two decades of experience in emergency services as both a nurse and firefighter, Jeremy has spent much of his professional life in environments where decisions must be made quickly and where accurately understanding a situation can have profound consequences. In these high-stakes settings, perception is not simply an abstract concept—it directly affects outcomes. What one person may see as chaos, another may recognize as an opportunity for decisive action. What appears threatening to one individual may be interpreted by another as a solvable challenge. Through years of working with patients, colleagues, and communities under pressure, Jeremy has developed a deep appreciation for how perception shapes behavior and decision-making.

This book takes readers on a thoughtful journey into the ways our perspectives are formed and how they influence nearly every aspect of our lives. Our upbringing, personal experiences, beliefs, and cultural influences all contribute to the lens through which we interpret the world. Too often, we move through life assuming that our view of reality is the objective truth. Yet, as Jeremy illustrates throughout this book, much of what we accept as "reality" is filtered through personal interpretation.

One of the most compelling aspects of this work is its emphasis on awareness. Jeremy challenges readers to pause and examine their own assumptions—the automatic interpretations that guide many of our daily interactions and decisions. By recognizing that perception is shaped rather than fixed, individuals gain the ability to reassess situations, approach conflicts with greater understanding, and make more thoughtful choices.

Throughout the book, Jeremy also explores the influence of power, control, and personal bias in shaping perception. These forces can subtly distort how we interpret situations and other people, sometimes leading to misunderstandings or unnecessary conflict. By becoming more mindful of these influences, readers can develop a clearer understanding of their own thinking and cultivate a more balanced and thoughtful perspective.

At its heart, *The Power of Perception* is both reflective and practical. It encourages readers not only to think differently but also to act differently. When individuals become aware of the lens through which they view the world, they gain the ability to adjust that lens. This shift can lead to improved communication, stronger relationships, and more effective leadership. It also fosters greater empathy, allowing us to appreciate that others may interpret the same circumstances through entirely different experiences.

In a time when misunderstandings and polarized viewpoints often dominate conversations, the message of this book is particularly timely. Jeremy reminds us that while we cannot control every situation we encounter, we do have the power to examine and refine the perspective through which we interpret those situations. That awareness alone can be transformative.

The Power of Perception offers readers a thoughtful reminder that understanding begins not only with observing the world around us but also with examining the assumptions within us. It is a compelling invitation to reconsider how we see, how we interpret, and ultimately how we respond to the world we share.

I believe you will find Jeremy Yates's insights both meaningful and practical as you begin this journey through the power of perception.

– Jeff Solheim
MSN, RN, CEN, CFRN, CBRN, TCRN, FAEN, FAAN

TABLE OF CONTENTS

PART 5: Uncovering the Illusion

INTRODUCTION

THE LENS WE LIVE THROUGH

We don't see the world as it is; we see it as *we* are.

Every day, we interpret moments, people, and circumstances through a lens built from our experiences, beliefs, fears, hopes, and histories. This lens is called **perception**, and it's a silent force shaping our thoughts, choices, behaviors, and even the direction of our lives.

You and I could witness the same event yet walk away with entirely different stories about what happened. Those stories influence what we feel, what we believe, and how we respond to the world around us. One person might see failure, while another sees a lesson. One might see disrespect, while another sees indifference. Neither is *wrong*, but neither is *universal*, either. That's the complexity, and the power, of perception.

My name is Jeremy, and I have a diverse background as both a nurse and a firefighter. Throughout my twenty-plus years in healthcare and the fire service, I have noticed that different perspectives can greatly influence our understanding of patient care. As a nurse, I worked in hospitals, often with critically ill patients. Then, just days after their discharge from the intensive care unit (ICU), I would respond to 911 calls in the community and encounter those same patients at home.

This experience highlighted a disconnect, a gap in continuity of care. In the hospital, I felt frustrated when patients returned for treatment shortly after their discharge, and, conversely, I felt frustrated in the field when I saw them struggling at home after just leaving a healthcare facility. This led me to question the reasons behind the disconnect.

I began to focus on what are now referred to as the "social determinants of health." These are the factors that impact an individual's health beyond just a medical diagnosis. While the term is increasingly familiar in the healthcare industry, simply dropping "health" and focusing on "social determinants" underscores that this subject shapes how we live, not just how healthy we are.

For instance, it's not enough to prescribe the right medication; we must consider whether the patient can afford it. Similarly, while we might suggest dietary changes, we should also ask if they can buy and cook the necessary foods. Throughout life, some people live for exotic vacations, while others are happy with time at home with family and friends. Some want expensive experiences, while others enjoy the company of the people around them.

This realization broadened my perspective on health and healthcare and eventually on the world around me. I continued to advance my career, earning a bachelor's degree in nursing, then a Doctor of Nursing Practice (DNP). My doctoral focus was on community leadership with a population health emphasis, which provided me with a comprehensive understanding of the healthcare system. In turn, I was able to see how these things impacted our daily lives, not just our health.

I gained insights into how political landscapes affect patient care, including regulations affecting hospitals and patient access. I saw how changes in Medicare and Medicaid coverage impacted access to healthcare. I also recognized how non-healthcare policies, such as redefining poverty-level income thresholds or laws around student loan access and forgiveness, can profoundly affect people's lives.

The more I learned, the more I noticed that these dynamics extend outside of healthcare. We often have bad days that affect our interactions, whether it's being short with a cashier or a server, yelling at a driver beside us on the road, or even deciding which activity to participate in or what food to eat. This pattern of behavior made me more aware of how our moods and circumstances can shape our perceptions and interactions with others and even the world around us.

Overall, I strive to view the world and my experiences through this lens of understanding, recognizing the broader themes in life. I decided to share my thoughts on this topic in hopes that we can start labeling people a little less, listening to them a little more, and building stronger relationships. I believe that relationships are essential for meaningful conversations in which we can truly listen to one another.

Listening doesn't mean that we always agree or believe the same things. Instead, it allows us to engage in the conversations necessary for moving forward. We might not see eye to eye all the time, but we can achieve understanding and mutual respect. We can learn and grow from each other's experiences.

Outside of healthcare, our interpretations of the world largely depend on our experiences. This is something we see throughout life. For instance, someone who has never faced food insecurity may not consider the practicalities of grocery shopping, such as which store to visit or what food they can afford. Additionally, a person who grew up worrying about where their next meal would come from is often less focused on healthy eating and more concerned with just having enough food.

In this book, we'll explore perception not just as a mental process but as a personal looking glass, a compass used to guide our course and navigate the journey of our daily lives. We'll investigate where it comes from, how it differs from person to person, and how it can distort or define our sense of reality.

But we won't stop there. Perception is just the foundation. With control over our perceptions, we gain the power to influence the world around us.

We will discuss how power comes with its own set of obstacles, starting with the common misperceptions we have about it: what it is, who has it, and how we obtain and use it. We will flip the script a bit and see how we typically think of power as control when, in reality, control over our perceptions is what leads to true power.

This journey will bring to light the misperceptions, chaos, and never-ending struggle of the power chase. Having a clear understanding of internal versus external power is a key component to gaining control over how we interpret and interact with the world.

This journey has six stages, with each step building on the last:

- **Perceiving perception**: Defining the term and seeing how it influences our interactions with the world around us.
- **Power**: Flipping the script by turning our definition and view of power upside down.
- **The power of perception**: Taking a look at how a realization of our perceptions and a new definition of power come together to provide a foundation for new possibilities.

- **Harnessing power**: Taking control of the controllable to obtain power and how we can use it wisely to create change in the world around us.
- **Uncovering the illusion**: Pulling back the curtain of our current understanding to gain new perspectives and successfully walk the tightrope.
- **Practical application**: A conclusion with next steps for how you can wield the power of perception in your everyday life to influence the world around you.

The Power of Perception isn't about changing the world; it's about changing how you see it and, in doing so, changing how you show up and interact with it. This book is an invitation to pause, reflect, and reconsider. To shift from reacting to choosing. To stop accepting the default lens handed to you by your past and start shaping a lens that serves your growth, truth, and power.

Let's begin.

CHAPTER 1

DEFINING PERCEPTION

What exactly is perception?

Interestingly, the definition of perception is filled with vague terms that don't necessarily clarify its meaning. This is because perceptions differ from person to person; we each have a unique lens through which we view the world. The challenge arises when we realize that our perception becomes our reality.

It's important to understand that our individual realities do not represent an objective reality. For example, someone who grows up without consistent access to food will have a very different view of food security and scarcity compared to someone who has never had to struggle for their next meal.

Understanding what perception means is the foundation for recognizing and regaining power over your views, thoughts, and actions. Start by thinking about what comes to mind when you hear the word "perception." You are likely thinking of how something is viewed.

At its simplest, perception is the way we interpret the world around us. It's how we make sense of what we see, hear, feel, and experience. But perception goes far beyond sensory input; it's also emotional, mental, and deeply personal. Two people can look at the same sunset, hear the same words, or face the same challenge, yet walk away with completely different understandings. That difference is perception.

Think of your favorite movie, one you watch over and over again. With whom have you shared the experience? Better yet, who did you watch it with, and did they seem to be as entertained as you? Now look at the movie reviews for it. Did the "expert" movie critics agree with you? It is the difference in perception that makes one person watch a movie over and over again while another person can't get through the opening credits.

Most definitions of perception focus on its role in gathering and interpreting sensory information. Psychologists define it as the process of recognizing and interpreting stimuli through our senses. But when we bring perception into the realm of real life, such as with relationships, decisions, and identity, it becomes much more than just data processing. It becomes our *story* about reality.

Talk to any child. Toddlers are my favorite. There is something about the honesty of a child between the ages of two and five. Ask them about anything you feel you know about and see what they have to say.

One of the best illustrations I've encountered regarding perception comes from observing my daughters. Even at a young age, they exhibited distinct perceptions and viewpoints. As they grew older, I could reflect on these differences in their behaviors.

My oldest daughter was born with an innate sense of what she could and could not do, which displayed a perception of limitations from a very early age. Even as a toddler, her attitude often translated to *I can't do this, so I won't even try*. This was evident in many situations throughout her early life. For example, during tummy time, she would cry because she preferred to play on her back rather than on her stomach.

I still vividly remember the first time I laid her down and how, amid her crying, she suddenly realized she could roll over.

My wife and I had known for a while that she could physically roll over, which sometimes left us feeling frustrated. We could see her potential, but she seemed determined to resist it.

After she discovered this ability, something clicked for her. She paused, surveyed the situation, and thought, *Okay, so this is how I solve the problem*. From that point on, every time we put her on her stomach, she would be halfway onto her back before we even had a chance to set her down completely.

I witnessed the same theme when she began to walk, showcasing her evolving perception and newfound confidence. Most babies go through a typical process when learning to walk. They start by pulling themselves up, looking around, and then letting go to clap for a moment before sitting back down. Eventually, they begin to toddle, reaching for support and taking a few steps before falling.

However, my oldest daughter was different. She decided to walk a little after her first birthday. My wife and I were aware that she could walk because she demonstrated all the signs: she could pull herself up and stand, and she had the strength to do so. We encouraged her to walk, but she hadn't done it before her birthday. Despite knowing she could, she seemed to believe that she couldn't walk.

The first time my oldest daughter took steps, she didn't just take one or two; she stood in the living room while my wife and I were in the kitchen and walked a dozen steps across the floor without us noticing. Once she realized we were watching and that her mom didn't have her camera ready to capture the moment, she turned, smiled at us, and immediately sat back down as if to say, "I appreciate the suggestion to walk, and I gave it a fair shot. But I'm going back to crawling now."

My youngest daughter, on the other hand, is quite different. She is very matter-of-fact. When she knows she can do something, she has no doubt about it. I've seen her confidence since she was a toddler.

For instance, one day, while driving home from preschool, she wanted to play a game where she would yell out a letter of the alphabet, and we would say words that started with that letter. She yelled out, "A!" and we said, "Aunt," "Alabama," and so on. Then she yelled out, "F!" I responded with "fun," "family," and "friends," when suddenly, from the backseat, I heard her say, "I know what starts with F: phone!"

I felt bad because she was so smart and confident. I tried to explain that "phone" actually starts with a P and an H, but I understood how she could be confused since PH makes an F sound. I thought I had clarified it when I heard a pause, but then she exclaimed, "I didn't say *pone*. I said phone! F-F-F-Phone!"

This was the same child who, during that stage in life, would ask me questions she already knew the answer to just to see if I would answer correctly. I remember being asked one day why the sky was blue. I knew this! I had learned about the sky throughout my science classes in school.

I went into an elegant yet simple explanation of the science behind how the sunlight reflects through the atmosphere and bounces off the gases in the ozone layer. After I was finished explaining the science of the answer, I was told very simply, "The sky is blue because God made it that way."

My perception was that the answer needed to be a complicated explanation of how the universe works. My daughter's perception was different and so much simpler. The sky was blue simply because it was created that way.

The Personal Filter

The point is, perception is not objective. It's filtered through everything you've ever lived through: your culture, family, traumas, and triumphs. Your fears, hopes, expectations, and memories shape what you notice, what you ignore, and how you assign meaning. Where you grew up, your family environment, your successes and failures throughout life, and your personal values and beliefs all work beneath the surface to shape how you interpret feedback.

This reflects the differences between my two daughters. My oldest daughter often won't try something if she believes she can't do it. Meanwhile, my youngest daughter is full of confidence and eagerly jumps into new challenges, sure that she can figure things out.

Think of perception like a pair of glasses. Everyone wears a unique pair, tinted by their life experiences. Some lenses filter out sunlight, so things aren't so bright. Others reflect colors in a way that lets people see hues they wouldn't normally be able to see. Some lenses simply redirect light so it hits a different spot in the eye, making the picture clearer. No matter the lenses, they color and reframe how we see the world. Like physical lenses, we wear our perceptions and worldviews so often that, most of the time, we don't even realize we're looking through them.

Pretend you have just been given enough money to plan your dream vacation. Where are you going, and who is coming? Are you going camping in the wilderness, relaxing on a beach, hitting the slopes, or heading to another country to learn about some new culture? Are you bringing family, friends, or just a good book? The answer depends on your perception of the world.

While camping in the wilderness and living off natural resources sounds like the way to go for some, others only see bug bites, wild animals, and no amenities. The beach is often seen as the place to be, but just mentioning it can make some people feel the sand creeping into every crevice. The slopes can be nice, but good luck bringing that person who is always cold. Visiting another country sounds fun to some. To others, you may as well have asked them to sit through a boring history class.

The point is, we all have different perceptions. Our unique experiences, knowledge, and beliefs constantly work behind the scenes to make us dream of places some people would find miserable and to draw us closer to people others may not tolerate.

Perception vs. Reality

You may have heard the phrase "Perception is reality," but this isn't quite accurate. Perception *feels* like reality, and we behave as though it is, but that doesn't mean it always reflects what's true. Our individual perception is definitely our reality, but it may not be the universal truth for others.

Go back to the examples above. Two children, very close in age, were raised in the same environment by the same parents. One was a bit more apprehensive and consistently talked herself out of opportunities because she didn't perceive her ability to succeed. The other was so full of confidence that she could correct you with the wrong information or a limited understanding just because she knew certain things to be true.

It was their internal beliefs and interpretations of the world around them that led each to take a different view of the same situation. One waited to walk until she was proficient enough to walk across the room. The other was so sure of herself that she made the mistakes along the way just to keep up with her sister and anyone else in her life because she "knew" she could.

Our perceptions and what's real to us are often filtered, edited, and distorted before they ever reach our conscious awareness. That doesn't make us flawed; it makes us human. Just like with different personalities and development timelines among siblings, our brains digest all sorts of information to make a decision without our full awareness of what is being taken in. Our brain is designed to protect, predict, and simplify, and perception is one of the tools it uses to do so.

Think about how you respond to things in your everyday life. For some of you, there isn't that much to think about. You make decisions seamlessly, seemingly without much thought. For others, you need to know every detail and its consequences so you can research and evaluate every possibility to find the perfect decision.

Our perceptions shape how we interpret the same information before making a decision. The result of the decision is where we find reality. For those who made the decision quickly, your reality is likely positive. Things worked out and were "good enough." For those who need to research, you are likely evaluating the outcome of your decision and looking for "something better."

Understanding perception and how each person has their own is a useful tool. Like any tool, however, it can become rusty if not frequently used and properly cared for. If we consistently mistake our perception for *the* truth rather than *our* truth, we risk living in echo chambers of assumption, bias, and misunderstanding. We risk creating the very environments and experiences others are trying to eliminate or escape.

Why It Matters

Understanding perception is the first step in reclaiming your power. If your actions, emotions, and decisions are driven by perception, knowing how perception works and when it's working against you is vital. Without understanding and accepting that your truth isn't *the* truth and that your perception may differ from that of others, you create separation. This separation is the beginning of a domino effect of damage.

On the other hand, being aware of the ways others may interpret the same experiences is the first step toward achieving togetherness and harmony. Realizing there are other points of view on the same situation helps us see through others' lenses.

Shutting down the idea that others have views different from ours creates division, separation, and destruction. When we recognize there are other possibilities, we begin to understand others, bridge relational gaps, and build each other up.

Neglecting others' perceptions will eventually leave us in an environment devoid of relationships and personal growth, while seeking others' perceptions will foster greater empathy and bring us to new heights.

In the chapters that follow, we'll dive deeper into how perception forms, why it differs from person to person, and how you can become more aware of your lens. But for now, remember this: Your perception isn't fixed. It can shift. It can expand. And it can be reshaped.

Perception is powerful, but what's more powerful is realizing you have a say in how it's shaped.

Reflection Questions

1. What personal experiences, such as your upbringing, culture, successes, or failures, are acting as "lenses" to shape the way you interpret the world?
2. Think about a belief you hold strongly about yourself, e.g., "I'm good at this" or "I'm not capable of that." How might your past experiences have shaped that perception?
3. In what areas of your life might you be mistaking your perception for objective truth? How could you challenge or re-examine that viewpoint?

CHAPTER 2

CONCEPTUALIZING PERCEPTION

Conceiving is believing!

By now, we know that perception is more than just passive observation. It's not merely what enters our senses; it's what our mind *does* with that information.

In this chapter, we take perception a step further. We explore how what we *conceive*, our inner thoughts, ideas, expectations, and beliefs, can actively *shape* what we perceive, and we examine how our experiences shape our interpretations.

Realizing there are different views has incredible power. However, we can't begin to recognize other views until we understand where our own views come from. Understanding that our beliefs, education, life experiences, personal opinions, relationships, and many other facets of our lives shape how we interpret the world around us is critical to taking the first step toward recognizing that our perceptions are truly our own.

Our view is not necessarily the same as someone else's. Whether our experiences have been positive or negative, what we have or have not experienced will determine our view of a situation. All these things shape the lens through which we view life. Each lens reflects light a little differently.

With glasses, there are many prescriptions to enable different people to see an image the same way. The lens of life has the opposite effect: our perceptions reshape the same image into different views. Two people can look at the same situation at the same time yet have completely different views, determined by how their lives have shaped their personal lenses on the world.

There is a common phrase, "Seeing is believing." This book aims to show you that reality is often quite the opposite: **believing is seeing**. This is seen most commonly in childhood. Children don't need to see Santa deliver presents to know he is real. They believe in the magic of the season, and that is enough to see the joy of the holiday and the imagination of endless possibilities.

This doesn't end when we become adults; rather, it shifts to bigger ideas. Adults will read news articles or listen to speakers and interpret, or "see," the message based on their own beliefs about reality.

Drawing from my introduction, I want to highlight a key epiphany I had over my twenty-plus years in healthcare, particularly in leadership roles. I often saw the same patients both in and out of the hospital, which revealed different perceptions among healthcare providers and patients themselves.

As an ICU nurse, I worked the night shift and cared for patients in the hospital. During the day, I would respond to emergency calls as a firefighter and emergency medical technician (EMT). On several occasions, I recognized patients while attending these 911 calls. In those situations, I would ask for their discharge folder, knowing they had been hospitalized recently. They would show me their folder, which contained information on healthy eating, weight management, medication adherence, and other critical advice.

From the perspective of the fire service, it was frustrating to see these patients calling 911 time and time again, especially after just receiving care in the hospital. As a nurse, I found it frustrating to see patients readmitted, knowing they weren't following the plan of care they'd been given. As a patient, it was frustrating for them not to have the ability to manage a condition and enjoy life.

This led me to various questions: Why were we being called if the hospital had already treated them? Why wasn't the patient better if they were just treated? Shouldn't the hospital have resolved the patients' issues? Didn't the patients want to be better? These questions and experiences inspired me to explore all sides of the healthcare lens.

In the hospital, we believed that we had done our part by providing care and facilitating recovery. However, we also recognized that the road to full recovery was ongoing, which required continued support beyond the hospital walls.

On the other hand, as first responders, we could only assist during emergencies. We often had to ask, "Is there something that needs to be addressed immediately? Do you need to return to the hospital?" This created frustration among all parties involved, including the patients.

Ultimately, this all shaped my graduate project for my doctorate degree. I focused on bridging the gap between in-hospital and out-of-hospital care. My research examined programs that were beginning to address these issues within hospital settings.

The program I studied during my project really exemplified the concept of "believing is seeing." My study targeted patients with heart failure. Team members of this program would actually visit patients in their homes to provide support, but it all began in the hospital.

The staff would express concerns, saying, "I'm not entirely sure this patient will have what they need when they return home. Can you come and speak with them?" They would agree, and a program representative would initiate a conversation at the hospital. Once the patient was discharged, they would follow up by calling: "Hey, when would be a good time for me to stop by?" The hospital even provided vehicles for the employees to facilitate these visits.

The program enabled staff to spend time with patients in their homes. For those with heart failure, critical topics included diet, exercise, and monitoring weight to prevent significant fluid retention or loss. This approach provided a clearer understanding of the patient's entire situation. As a result, they could reduce excessive 911 calls and prevent hospital readmissions.

By offering resources and meeting patients where they are, they have made a significant impact. Again, this healthcare analogy goes well beyond simply getting healthy. I truly believe that addressing people in their environment and space is essential for fostering open conversations, enhancing understanding, and improving overall interactions in our society.

During home visits, staff would ask patients, "Do you have a scale to accurately weigh yourself daily? It's crucial to monitor fluid intake through weight, as this is an early sign of congestive heart failure getting better or worse." They learned about the patients' community resources and access to food. Collaborating with community partners, they helped patients overcome barriers.

If food access were an issue, they might connect patients with food banks or similar services. They would inquire, "Who takes you to your doctor's appointments? Who helps you with grocery shopping?" Historically, grocery stores didn't offer delivery services, so for those unable to go out, fast-food restaurants were often the only option. If a patient relies on fast food and cannot access a grocery store, asking them to maintain a healthy diet becomes nearly impossible. Today, with delivery services like DoorDash, Uber Eats, and Grubhub, access to food has improved, but this evolution has taken time.

The Mind's Role in Percepti on

Our brains are not neutral observers of reality. They are constantly building and remodeling reality. In fact, the mind anticipates what we expect to see before we fully experience it. That's why two people standing side by side can walk away from the same moment with entirely different takeaways. Their *internal concepts* (what they experience, believe, expect, or fear) filled in the gaps and colored the experience before it was fully formed.

In Chapter 1, we talked about how our experiences become the "lenses" we use to view the world. Our experiences program our mind's algorithm for creating outcomes and keeping us safe. They shape our beliefs, our desires, and our dreams. Often, our minds use past experiences to process information and reach a conclusion before it actually happens. Our experiences are the lens that bends and reflects the information around us, creating the final image we see.

For example, if you mostly observe people being selfish and giving little thought to others, you likely have formed the belief that people are generally selfish, and you might even feel uneasy or cautious when interacting with "nice" people. If you believe people are generally selfish, your mind will zero in on the moments that confirm that belief.

On the contrary, if you have been able to look at events in life as opportunities for new adventures and new people, you may likely be anchored in a belief that change is good and "bad" things are just opportunities for improvement or new experiences. If you believe the world is full of opportunities, you'll notice chances others miss. This isn't just a matter of positive thinking or negativity bias; it's perception shaped by conception.

Expectations Become Filters

Psychologists call this "top-down processing." Your brain takes what it already *knows* (or thinks it knows) and uses that to interpret incoming information. It's a shortcut that helps you make fast judgments, but it also means you're rarely seeing things as they are. You're seeing them as you *expect* them to be. This is great when you need to quickly swerve your car to avoid hitting something, but not so great when you meet someone new.

You are probably familiar with phrases like "A first impression is a lasting one" or "You never get a second chance at a first impression." These speak to human nature to use our past experiences to form quick judgments. Why are first impressions so meaningful? Because they create the foundation for how we will continue to interpret and interact with this person for the rest of our lives.

The issue with this is that people change. If we consistently use our subconscious to judge people, we don't always recognize when they change.

We do this naturally in daily life. Think about how often we walk into a room with a pre-decided opinion. A meeting, a date, a conversation—our expectations set the tone. When meeting new people, we begin by dissecting how they are dressed, their title or position, and the way they present themselves before a word is even spoken. For a meeting or event, we consider the venue and the people involved to determine what to say or do before we even get there.

Before a single word is spoken, we've already formed a narrative in our head: *This won't go well; she's probably judging me; I'm not good at this.* And once we've conceived that story, our perception tends to reinforce it. This all happens through the lens of our experience. If we haven't had positive interactions with meeting new people or trying new things, we have feelings of fear and anxiety before ever trying.

Conversely, if we have had positive experiences, we feel joy and excitement as we look forward to the possibility of success. Feedback can become criticism, and we can cast aside people who can really add value to our lives, or it can become peace and joy when we see the possibility of the positive. Our experiences shape how we interpret feedback, which can either lead us to respond defensively and alienate ourselves from others, or show up with honesty and create something wonderful we never even imagined.

Belief as a Creative Force

Our beliefs don't stop at our mental awareness or quick decision-making. What we conceive mentally often manifests physically. Athletes visualize their wins. Artists see their creations before making them. Leaders envision success before they inspire others to pursue it. Perception, when consciously shaped, becomes a *creative tool.*

When we believe in a possibility, our minds search for evidence to support it. When we want a goal, we take steps to achieve it. We become more open, receptive, resilient, and persevering. The opposite is also true: when we believe in limitations, our perception will bend reality to fit that limitation. We will keep ourselves from success, or even trying, because we know it just won't work.

Let's go back to the example in Chapter 1 of the difference between my oldest and youngest child to see this in practice. With my oldest daughter, her self-imitations didn't stop at rolling over or when to walk. They continue to be something she has to overcome to try new things.

My youngest daughter is still full of confidence. For her, it is about helping her see areas where she needs to grow and learn more or helping her understand old topics at much deeper levels. My oldest daughter will struggle to try new things when she is unsure and needs encouragement, while my youngest daughter jumps right in but needs encouragement to pull back a bit, to pause and learn.

That's why awareness is everything. If we don't question our concepts about ourselves, others, and the world, we risk letting outdated or distorted beliefs rule our lives. Questioning ourselves helps keep us from being stuck in the past and from limiting our future. Things change. New studies, new experiences, and new people should all change how we perceive the world.

If you can honestly say you have not changed from five or even ten years ago, you are limiting yourself. The world has changed. New ideas and information have been presented. We should constantly question the world and ourselves. Without questioning, there is no growth. We become antiquated and outdated. Our perceptions become limitations.

Rewriting the Script

You have the power to reframe what you conceive. You can choose different beliefs, entertain new perspectives, and open yourself to seeing the same world through a new lens, just like you can choose a different pair of glasses to help you read or even see the world around you better. This doesn't mean ignoring pain or pretending everything is positive. It means recognizing that your *starting point*, your internal conception, sets the direction of your perception.

The beginning of rewriting your script is to recognize that there are other possibilities, then question them and be open to the possibility of change. Recognize the mind's will to form opinions without all the information, and take a breath before meeting a new person or going to that event. Don't ignore new ideas and information. Instead, compare it with what you know and other sources of information to see if it makes sense. Open yourself to the idea that you can and will evolve.

It's not just about changing *what* you see. It's about changing *how* you *see*. Your physical eyes don't change. Your mental processing of the information will. Life should feel a bit like grocery shopping. It's always the same choice, but you make different decisions each week. You will always have the same ingredients in life, but what you choose to make with them will change.

In the next chapter, we'll bring these ideas to life. We'll explore how people interpret the *same* event in radically *different* ways and what that reveals about the incredible complexity and possibility of perception.

Reflection Questions

1. Think about a belief you hold strongly about the world or other people. How might that belief influence the way you interpret everyday situations?
2. What is one situation in your life in which your perception of an event or person turned out to be different from what you originally thought? What shaped your interpretation? How might the experience have been different if your expectations were different?
3. In what area of your life might an old belief or assumption be limiting how you see new possibilities? What might happen if you questioned that belief?

CHAPTER 3

PERCEPTION IN PRACTICE

Perceiving is seeing.

Our personal experiences play a significant role in how we perceive the world around us. For example, when walking down the street and encountering a stranger, our feelings of safety or threat can differ greatly. Someone who has experienced an attack may feel threatened regardless of the situation, while a person accustomed to busy streets may feel at ease around strangers. Thus, our reactions to similar scenarios can vary widely.

When discussing various social determinants of life, a common activity is "the line game." In this game, participants line up against a wall in a room, each with one hand on the wall. They stand in a starting position with one hand touching the wall and then respond to statements or questions posed by the facilitator. If a statement applies to them, they take a step forward; if it doesn't apply, they either stay in place or step back.

For instance, if the facilitator asks whether anyone grew up in a home with a computer or smartphone, those who did would step forward, while those who did not would stay put or step back. The questions vary, often focusing on academic achievements, such as the degree held, GPA, or having access to tutoring. By the end of the game, some participants may find themselves near the finish line on the opposite side of the room, while others remain close to the starting point, highlighting the disparities in experiences and opportunities.

The goal is to provide a different perspective on how various factors influence our interactions and the advantages and disadvantages we encounter in the world. Even from the outset, it's evident that someone with longer arms has a better head start than someone with shorter arms, highlighting disparities in experiences.

Imagine taking a group of friends to your favorite restaurant. They have never been, but you have been telling them for years that this place has the best burgers. You order your favorite burger and fries for everyone. After the meal, you feel a sense of satisfaction, but one of your friends gives you a "meh" and says it was just okay. Later that night, another one of your friends gets sick.

Three completely different responses. The food didn't change, but the experience of it did. Why? Because everyone has their own way of interpreting things. Interpreting taste comes from an array of different sources, such as taste buds, smell, and texture. While everyone had the same input (burgers), they were *filtering* it through their own body chemistry. Just like this physical process, our perceptions are constantly *filtered* through our experiences and beliefs.

This is perception in practice. It's the realization that even when we share an experience, we don't *share* an experience; we don't all perceive it the same way. We each live in our own internal world constructed by our unique experiences, memories, emotions, identities, and meanings. This is why perception is so powerful and why misunderstanding is so common. It is incredibly difficult to see things through the lenses of others.

Perception Is Personal

Every interpretation of reality is personal. Let's take a simple example: a boss sends a brief email that says, *"See me in my office."* One employee immediately worries, assuming they're in trouble. Another feels excited, thinking they're going to be recognized for a job well done. A third feels indifferent; it's just another meeting.

Same message. Same words. Three completely different emotional reactions. What's changed? Not the message but the *lens* through which it was received.

That lens is formed over time. It's shaped by:

- **Past experiences**: *Have I been praised or punished in similar situations?*
- **Core beliefs**: *Do I believe I'm capable? Respected? Safe?*
- **Emotional state**: *Am I anxious, confident, or burnt out?*
- **Cultural background**: *What does authority mean to me?*

This is how perception makes reality feel so *real,* even when it's completely different for each person. How we have experienced life up to this point will shape the lens through which we view the world.

It is natural to gravitate toward people who see things the same way we do. Human nature makes us long for companionship and validation. We want friends who enjoy the same things we do. Having people in our lives who share our beliefs and life experiences, good or bad, validates our opinions and feelings.

While this isn't inherently bad, it creates an "autopilot" mode in life where we struggle to step outside our comfort zones and see different perspectives. We put on the same pair of glasses every day to look at the world and choose how to interact with it. Having the same view creates a cycle of the same decisions: if it happened this way before, it will happen this way again. If someone broke my trust, then I might believe that everyone else will, too. If I never had to worry about finding food to eat in the past, I would not naturally worry about my next meal.

One of my favorite activities showcasing this idea is an impromptu bingo game I created while teaching at the fire department. We were discussing social determinants of health, and to emphasize this concept, I designed the game. Each firefighter received a bingo card filled not with numbers but with life events. For example, events included statements like "I have been arrested," "I didn't know where my next meal was going to come from," and "I have had my car repossessed." If someone had experienced it, they could not mark their card. In contrast, if they lacked the experience, they could check off the item.

The outcome of the game was remarkable and effectively demonstrated the key point. One firefighter in particular, who had endured many struggles growing up, consistently found himself unable to mark off his boxes. Finally, a participant with fewer hardships ended up winning. After the game, the firefighter who faced numerous challenges looked at me and remarked, "If we had played it the other way around, I would have won ten items ago," highlighting how our experiences in life can make the same goal harder to obtain for some.

This reinforces the idea that our experiences shape how we navigate the world. For instance, if we grow up in environments where trust is scarce, we are conditioned to be wary. When we encounter someone unfamiliar on the street, our past experiences could lead us to react defensively or avoid them altogether. This encapsulates how our backgrounds and experiences not only create advantages and disadvantages but also influence our perceptions of the world.

How do you feel about the firefighter who "should have won"? Your reaction may range from sadness over his circumstances to guilt for recognizing the advantages you have had compared to others' disadvantages, or even anger at how differently the world treats people.

The Same Storm, Different Boats

There's a saying: "We're all in the same storm but not in the same boat." Some boat captains are experienced and confident in sailing through storms; they can navigate challenging weather conditions. In contrast, others may avoid sailing at all at the first sign of clouds. These differences stem from their life experiences, such as how long they have been sailing, the type of boat they operate, and the number of storms they have encountered.

This metaphor applies to life as well. We all face our own "storms," and the number and severity of past challenges influence how we handle future difficulties. It perfectly captures the idea that life may throw similar challenges at us, such as loss, uncertainty, success, and change, but how we respond is colored by our inner frameworks.

For example:

- A breakup may devastate one person and liberate another.
- Losing your job could be seen as incompetence and failure or as a fresh start and a new adventure.
- Public speaking might trigger panic in one and excitement in another.

The event alone doesn't determine the outcome. *Perception does.*

Why It Matters

Understanding that perception is personal helps us in two major ways:

1. **It creates empathy**: We stop assuming everyone sees what we see or reacts how we would. This reduces judgment and opens space for deeper connection.
2. **It creates awareness**: We begin to question our automatic responses. *Is what I'm feeling based on fact or my interpretation of it?*

This awareness is the gateway to growth. When we recognize that we're not always reacting to *reality* but to our *version* of it, we reclaim the ability to choose differently. Recognizing that there are other possibilities helps us understand and connect with others. Recognizing that there are other realities allows us to see things through other people's lenses and share in their experiences. In turn, we make meaningful connections, allowing us to share our reality and experiences and strengthen ourselves and those around us.

Perception in Relationships and Conflict

Many arguments are rooted not in what happened, but in *how it was perceived*. If you have had any type of relationship with another person (romantic, child-parent), you have likely had the argument, "It's not *what* you said; it's *how* you said it!" Your nonverbal language speaks volumes more than your words.

The hardest part of this truth is the fact that nonverbal communication is up to the receiver to interpret. When two people disagree, walking away for a bit to think is a common tactic. Upon reconvening, however, one person says, "You ignored me," while the other replies, "I was giving you space." Both may be telling the truth from their perspective.

When we fail to acknowledge perception's role, we think we are arguing about facts. In reality, we are arguing about our personal perceptions of those facts. When we learn to see perception as fluid, we begin to ask better questions: "What did you see?" "How did that feel to you?" "What were you expecting?"

These kinds of questions open the door to mutual understanding, not necessarily agreement but respect. People want to be heard and respected. Most people can accept disagreements as long as they feel they have been heard and respected.

When you recognize that your reality is not necessarily *the* reality, you can shift your conversation toward others' thoughts and feelings, creating a space where they can feel heard and respected.

Practice: Observing Perception in Real Time

You can begin practicing this awareness by doing the following:

- Notice your immediate emotional reactions. What belief might they be connected to?
- When something upsets you, ask: *What story am I telling myself about this?*
- In a disagreement, pause and say: *This may look different from their point of view. Let me ask instead of assuming.*

We've now seen how perception operates in real time, how it shapes what we feel, think, and do. But perception doesn't exist in isolation. It interacts with another human driving force: **power**.

In the next section, we'll shift our focus to understanding power: what it is, how we seek it, and how it can spiral into chaos when misunderstood.

Reflection Questions

1. When you receive a short message, criticism, or unexpected feedback, what assumptions do you tend to make first? How might those assumptions influence your reaction?
2. How do the people you surround yourself with reinforce or challenge your current perceptions about the world?
3. The next time you experience conflict or misunderstanding, what is one question you could ask to better understand the other person's perception before reacting?

CHAPTER 4

DEFINING POWER

What is power?

It's a word that evokes emotion. We often think of power as the ability to control something or someone by force or coercion. For some, it means control. For others, influence. Many think of royal families and the lineages of kings, queens, and emperors. Or maybe they think of their boss at work or the person running the company. Still others think of dominance, control, and submission.

The truth is that power is more than a title, position, or control. Power is the influence we have over our relationships and decisions in every interaction. Power is the ability to bring people together or create division. It's the difference between trying to force your beliefs on others and challenging your own views, choosing to find comfort in their truth or to grow as you evolve as a person. Redefining power as an internal rather than an external force is the foundation for gaining true power.

One area of confusion regarding power is the distinction between power and control. This dynamic is often evident in a boss-report relationship. We tend to assume that someone with a title automatically has authority or power over others.

What we want to clarify is that it's not just about having authority over someone; it's about understanding where we typically see power. The crucial point is the difference between feeling powerful and feeling powerless. This distinction shifts our mindset, potentially changing our perception. That's why discussing and defining power is so important.

Power Defined

At its essence, **power is the ability to influence or affect outcomes**. Influence can be gained through authority (your boss told you to do it, so you will) or by charisma (your favorite movie star goes to a restaurant, and now you want to go). This influence can be external, impacting others, situations, or environments, or internal, shaping how we think, feel, and act. Power isn't inherently good or bad. It is a neutral force shaped by how we choose to use it. What matters is *how* it's used, *why* it's desired, and *what* it's rooted in.

Power comes in various forms. Some of the most common types of power are:

- **Structural/Institutional**: Direct power to enact and enforce rules, laws, and regulations. Most commonly, this is a typical business or government structure. People are put into positions to create and enforce rules and laws that others must follow.
- **Social**: Often coveted outside of business and industry. This is commonly seen by "social influencers" who are popular in society. Social power focuses on status or relationships. Social power is what makes us want something just because someone else wants it, or to be included in a relationship. Wanting a bigger house, a faster car, and designer clothes because we see influencers, movie stars, and athletes with them is due to social power.

- **Personal**: The internal power we have over ourselves. Throughout the next chapters, we will discuss this as "true" power. This is our control over what we do and say. Personal power is when we respond with empathy rather than anger, properly budget our finances, apologize when we hurt someone, and do everything else we think, say, and do.
- **Perceived**: Taking away our power and giving it to others. It is the *belief* in someone's power that leads us to act as if it is true. This is what makes us change how we act and who we are, depending on the person we are interacting with. We see someone get out of an exotic car wearing an Italian suit, and we perceive that they have money, status, and influence. This perception changes how we treat them. When we do this, we are actually giving away our power by allowing others to control us.

Perceived power is dangerous because it is active. Structural and social powers are tangible. Your boss really can fire you. Our government really does enact and enforce laws we must follow. Advertisements will never stop because people all over the world still spend money on shoes just because they see famous athletes wearing them.

Personal and perceived power are opposing internal powers: one gives us actual power, while the other takes it away and gives it to someone else. Personal power relies on self-awareness and self-acceptance to build internal strength through self-control. When we change our behavior, perceived power erodes our actual power by giving others control over us, not because they actually have power, but simply because we think they do.

Power over self is crucial to getting desired outcomes in life. Our perceptions control our outcomes. By taking control of our perceptions, we can control perceived power and exalt personal power.

Power vs. Control

A common misconception is that power equals control. While power *can* include control, they're not the same. Control is often about certainty and predictability. Power, on the other hand, is about *capacity*: your ability to respond, influence, or adapt. Power is about ability, while control is about restraint.

We see this most often in the political landscape of democracy. Lawmakers have the authority to create, enact, and enforce many types of laws to help others. With this type of power, why does it seem so often that a law aimed at making things better can actually make things worse? The answer is that political leaders have the power to make and enforce laws, but they have no control over how people respond to them.

We often hear about this issue in history class when talking about Prohibition. Alcohol was bad. Really bad. It caused declining health, destruction, and even death. The American government decided to make it illegal, intending to remove something harmful and actively help the people. They had the power to pass the law and have the police enforce it, but no control over citizens' response.

The result? Even more death and destruction because they couldn't control the people. The American people wanted their alcohol so badly that they went around the law to get it. The police couldn't keep up with the rising crime rate, so the law was overturned. While the government had the ability to make alcohol illegal and have the police enforce it, they had no control over how the citizens would respond.

An example of this in today's society is the student loan crisis in the United States. The history of student loans provides a clear picture of power dynamics. Back in the late 1980s and early 1990s, college enrollment was declining, and schools sought help from politicians and the government. The solution they proposed was that students could take out loans to pay for college, enabling them to graduate from high school and attend college immediately, rather than working to save money first.

The government responded by using its power to guarantee student loans, allowing students to borrow money for their education and repay it after graduation, once they obtained better-paying jobs. Lawmakers decided to create and approve laws granting loans to anyone who wanted to attend college, regardless of any discriminatory factors (age, income, credit score, etc.), a grand idea aimed at promoting equality in access to higher education and advancement in career and life.

With such a noble cause, why is there considered to be a "crisis" with student loan debt? Lawmakers couldn't control how the loans were used by the people, the banks that funded the loans, or the colleges that provided the education. A combination of high interest rates, rising college tuition costs, and the lack of guaranteed employment has led many people to struggle to keep up with college loan debt.

Studies have shown that while this helped increase college enrollment, it also led to higher tuition prices. The days when a couple of thousand dollars could cover a year's expenses are long gone, and now we often hear about astronomical college costs of $40,000 to $50,000 per year at some high-end institutions. While the government had the power to decide what was legal, it had no control over the response.

To illustrate my point with a specific example, as a nurse, I have personal experience with student loan policies. On average, a nurse graduates from college and enters their first job with approximately $23,000 to $50,000 in student loan debt (NerdWallet 2024) and an initial salary of around $70,000 (Nurse.org 2023). These figures can vary a bit each year and by resource, but the bottom line is that an average nursing graduate typically starts off with debt equal to half their annual salary.

If you subtract the debt, nurses are making around minimum wage for a career that requires a college degree, licensing, and responsibility for people's lives. Even worse, nurses are needed now more than ever. After reading this, what is your perception of going to college and becoming a nurse?

When we look at the bigger picture, we see that many people use student loans to obtain degrees that do not guarantee employment. Imagine graduating with $20,000 to $50,000 in student loan debt and not being able to find a job in your field. While having access to money may have made someone feel powerful when choosing their degree and school, the combination of student loan debt and uncertain employment can leave them feeling pretty powerless.

The intent behind providing student loans was to help people gain higher education and better job opportunities. However, it has led to greater control over graduates. Students who go to college on the foundation of student loans now face mounting debt before they even begin their careers. The need to pay off this debt limits choices, as students must find and maintain a steady source of income to make the required loan payments.

Again, the government attempted to help by creating a policy offering relief to those in much-needed career fields or working in areas where finding willing workers is incredibly difficult. Either scenario aims to give people more power by expanding their choices but ultimately limits their power by forcing them to choose between debt to start a career or working in environments they would not have preferred just to earn income.

Exercising power to give access to money was noble. However, the lack of control has led to higher college tuition costs and debt, while reducing the number of people seeking higher education to start a career.

When we define power only as authority and dominion over others, we limit ourselves. True power often begins with the ability to *master oneself*. Constantly chasing the illusion of public power distracts us from the true power we have over our thoughts, emotions, and actions. Why chase the illusion of power over others if you truly have no control over the results when you can focus inward and gain real power through self-awareness and self-control?

You may not control your circumstances, but you can control your response. That's power. You may not control others' actions, but you can choose how they affect your self-worth. That's power. You may not control the harsh reality often associated with society, but you can choose to treat others with kindness and empathy. That's power.

Where Power Comes From

Just like perception, power arises from many sources, including:

- **Knowledge**: When you understand something deeply, you gain power over confusion and fear.
- **Choice**: The freedom to make decisions, even small ones, restores a sense of agency.
- **Perspective**: A new way of seeing things can change everything, even when nothing else changes.
- **Connection**: Power often comes from who you're with, not just who you are.
- **Perception**: How powerful you *believe* you are often shapes how powerful you *are*.

When we overlook these sources, we risk chasing only the *visible* forms of power, such as titles, wealth, and dominance, while ignoring the deeper, quieter forms that often matter more. Chasing the illusion of external power keeps us from the reality of internal power.

The Feeling of Powerlessness

Power is the antithesis of this negative feeling of powerlessness, which is why it is often seen as positive. Everyone knows what it feels like to be powerless. It's the moment you feel unheard, unseen, or stuck. It's when your choices feel limited or meaningless. If the opposite is to have and exert control, then power must be the better solution, right? Not exactly. The truth is: **feeling powerless is not the same as *being* powerless**.

We all have power waiting for us to claim, just not always the way the world tells us. Sometimes, power is dormant, not absent. It's hidden beneath layers of fear, doubt, or disconnection. One of the most liberating shifts in life is realizing that power is not something others give you; it's something you give yourself.

In the next chapter, we'll look at what drives people to *chase* power: the internal and external forces that make power such a persistent human obsession. You'll begin to see how the *quest for power*, when disconnected from awareness and perception, can lead to imbalance and chaos.

Reflection Questions

1. Think about a time when you felt powerless in a situation. Looking back, was there any personal power you still had that you might have overlooked at the time?
2. In what areas of your life might you be giving away your personal power by assuming someone else has more control than they actually do?
3. What is one situation in your life right now where focusing on your response rather than trying to control the outcome could change how you experience it?

CHAPTER 5

THE CONSTANT QUEST FOR POWER

Power is a fundamental human desire.

We often perceive power as a commodity, something we can acquire. It provides us with a sense of validation and authority, giving us a feeling of dominion over others. However, this chapter highlights a crucial realization: the more we pursue power, the more we find ourselves yearning for it. This pursuit creates an endless cycle. We believe that if we can just obtain "this" thing, we will be satisfied. Yet, once we achieve it, we immediately long for the next milestone.

You can observe this pattern in workplace environments. For instance, someone might think, *If I can just move up from the mailroom to another floor, I'll be happy.* Once they reach that goal, they may then set their sights on becoming a supervisor, and after that, a manager. The cycle continues as they strive to reach higher positions, such as becoming a director, and so on.

While seeking power isn't inherently *bad,* it is important to ensure you are chasing the right kind of power. Embarking on the wrong quest leaves undesired results. Think of any movie where the plot is chasing after a treasure. One person seeks it out to find answers about the story and share them with others, while another wants the fame and money associated with it. Which one usually wins? At the end of the movie, the person with noble intentions usually ends up with the coveted treasure (and giving it away somehow solves all their money problems). They even realize they enjoyed the quest and the learning experience right before the credits roll.

This relentless quest isn't limited to work; it permeates our everyday lives. Take the example of smartphones: why do we feel the need to upgrade to a new iPhone or Galaxy each year? The truth is, we don't necessarily need these upgrades, but we feel compelled to chase after the latest models. Each new smartphone has enticing features that draw us in, prompting us to buy the latest version for improved camera quality, increased memory, or enhancements for our social media content.

From ancient civilizations to modern society, people have fought for power, whether in the form of wealth, status, control, or influence. We read about the kings, queens, and rulers in history books. Each one has a massive kingdom of land, people, and wealth. But the quest for power isn't just about material gain or authority; it's often about something much deeper: a desire to feel significant, secure, and in control of one's environment.

In these stories, there was usually a fall after a quest for immortality or constant remembrance. Egyptian pharaohs built pyramids, kings and queens built statues, emperors built entire civilizations dedicated to their reigns, and civil rights pioneers who sacrificed their lives to correct the world's moral compass are honored with murals.

We are social creatures, hardwired to seek out ways to improve our position in the world. According to the modern societal view of power, it is, well, powerful. It's an escape. It's liberating. It brings freedom. It's control over our circumstances and destinations, over the people and things around us. By controlling outside aspects of our lives, we control our destiny. With the right title, enough money, or over a million likes, we can do anything!

This common view of power is what makes it so dangerous. This view holds that power is gained by taking it. In reality, the more we chase power, the more we give up. Titles can be gone in an instant. Money can only buy so much, and eventually, the likes will move on to the next viral post.

The truth is, power is internal. Power is the ability to not let your external circumstances control you or your view of life. Power is taking a different perspective and keeping yourself out of the power chase. There is nothing wrong with having titles, money, or status. The problem lies in viewing these things as the source of power and getting caught in the never-ending chase.

Starting the Power Quest

Every journey, every quest, has a beginning. Typically, it all starts with someone searching to find something they don't have. No matter the object or end goal, it serves to fill a void. People go on journeys to get something they don't have but desperately want: a new adventure, a love interest, or any number of other things.

We are prone to seek what we don't have, and power is no different. From the time we are born, we are powerless. We rely on our parents for food and safety. In adolescence, things don't get any easier when we seek independence through validation from others. Adulthood continues the same pattern, with the choice of the right career and the desire to make a mark on the world we leave behind.

As babies, we are taught to do tricks for validation. We roll over, crawl, walk, and talk because our parents praise us when we do. The only thing that changes as we get older is the shift in our circle of validation. It starts with our parents. Your career may even be the result of seeking parental validation by making them happy. Then approval comes from coworkers and bosses.

What is becoming more common is the need to seek validation on social media through likes, clicks, and shares.

But what happens when power becomes a need rather than a choice? When the quest for power is fueled by fear, it becomes an insatiable hunger. We start believing that power is the solution to all our problems, that if we just *had* enough, we'd be safe, fulfilled, or loved. And so, the cycle continues. Many people have gone on to write songs and books about how they finally achieved their "power" and still continue to have the problems they thought would go away. External power didn't fix their problems after all.

The issue with this is that no amount of external power can resolve internal insecurities. When we believe that power is the answer to our deepest fears, we constantly chase something that will never truly provide satisfaction. The more we get, the more we want, likely because the more we get, the more we realize it doesn't give us any control. As this cycle goes on, want turns to need. The reality is that the more we *need* power, the less control we have over our lives.

Power as Validation

For many, power is synonymous with validation. If we have power, if we can make people listen to us, respect us, or obey us, we feel seen, acknowledged, and valued. The validation that comes with power reinforces our sense of worth and importance. If people listen to what we say without rebuttal, it must mean they respect and agree with it, right?

However, this external validation is fleeting. Why do you think it is called a chase? Because seeking external validation is never-ending. It always leaves you wanting more.

Numerous studies have shown that different forms of validation can cause chemical reactions in the body. In essence, validation, in all its forms, causes the body to react as if it were taking a substance. The more validation we receive, the more our body reacts. More reaction leads to a new normal. This means the body needs the validation to continue so that the body can keep up the new normal.

Validation has the same effect on the body as other substances society warns against. You are likely able to replace validation with several other toxins you have seen in yourself or others around you. Seeking external validation has the same effect on the body as any other addictive substance: the more we get, the more we need. We begin to change who we are and how we act just to achieve validation. Eventually, we may not even recognize who we are because we have been so busy conforming just to seek external validation.

The Dark Side of the Power Chase

The relentless pursuit of power can lead to a number of negative consequences, both for ourselves and others:

- **Exhaustion and burnout**: The constant chase for more leaves us mentally, emotionally, and physically drained. As described earlier, the power chase is a never-ending quest in which the finish line keeps moving farther the more you chase it.
- **Relationships suffer**: When power is the primary goal, personal connections can become transactional. We begin using people to achieve our personal goals rather than connecting with them. Eventually, this will alienate people from us altogether.
- **Corruption of values**: In the pursuit of power, we may compromise our ethics, make selfish decisions, or betray our core beliefs. Even worse, our actions may override our previously held values, making these negative

cultural norms our own and allowing them to guide us through life. Our relationship with ourselves is lost.

- **Isolation**: The more power we chase, the more isolated we can become. The belief that only we can do something often separates us from the very people who could help. The belief that we don't need or can't accept help leads to alienation. Alienation turns to isolation, which has been linked to depression, hopelessness, and despair.

Getting the right start in the power chase is crucial. When power is sought to hide or overcome fear, anxiety, or insecurity, or to achieve a level of ego status, it causes destruction. Having the wrong perspective on power leads to a never-ending chase that can take the very thing away we are trying to achieve. With the wrong goal, the power chase leaves us powerless and blind to what really matters. It can even change who we are.

The Dream of Permanent Power

The most dangerous aspect of the power chase is the dream that we will permanently achieve it and hold on to it. We often live as if our job or title will never be lost because we are too integral to the company, our friends and family can't live without us, or our popularity won't fade.

Unfortunately, the truth is that power is transient. A merger, downsizing, failed project, or missed deadline can take away titles and jobs in an instant. While we have the ability to leave a lasting impression on the people around us, life always goes on. Popularity is only as constant as the latest trend or algorithm. On the surface, it seems sad, but this truth is actually quite freeing.

We see this throughout world history and even into today. Alexander the Great, Julius Caesar, and Adolf Hitler all sought power through the expansion of their empires. All caused massive destruction on their quest for power, control, and domination. All are gone, with their empires now much different from when they were in their power quests.

We see this even more rapidly in today's society. Movie stars, athletes, and influencers rise to popularity and create a global following, only to have their glory recede as soon as they say or do something that goes against the grain of society. One wrong opinion voiced, one bad news report, one allegation, and their career becomes a shadow of what it once was.

A good example is the movie *Gladiator*, which draws from events in ancient Rome while presenting a fictionalized version of that history. In the film, we observe Roman civilization, governed by an emperor. They constructed districts and established a great democracy, eventually becoming a world superpower.

However, as politicians and ordinary people rose to political office, they became corrupted by power. They pursued it so far that they felt they could not give it up. Consequently, they became more willing to distract the populace. Wars, political speeches, and games are all aimed at distracting the people and keeping politicians in their seats.

This distraction is a key theme in *Gladiator*, where the creation of gladiatorial games serves to divert people's attention from wars and other issues they are facing. In the movie, this cycle of distractions continues until someone intervenes. Marcus Aurelius, a great soldier who lost his family while away at war, steps in to halt the power struggle. However, the existence of a sequel suggests that the cycle repeats itself, reflecting real-life events.

While cinema is easy to dismiss as made up, we can also observe this pattern across various civilizations throughout history. For example, the ancient Aztecs and Mayans built vast empires, but today their once-thriving societies are often viewed as ancient ruins or artifacts. While these cultures have not completely disappeared, this serves as a reminder of how the pursuit of power leads to an endless cycle.

Next came Mesopotamia. Then the Greeks and Romans. Before Rome, there were the ancient Greeks. Each was once a powerful empire that sought to expand its territory. Yes, each civilization often overextended itself in its quest for more land, either scaling back to a more realistic level or being overtaken by a stronger power. Ancient Greece was eventually subdued by Rome.

Rome and Greece still exist, but they are a far cry from the empires we study in history books. Julius Caesar and Alexander the Great are credited with building vast empires that spanned modern-day countries and continents. The end result? These rulers are gone, and the empires they built are smaller versions of what they established.

In the present, we read every day about people who were simply living their lives when they experienced sudden, life-altering events. You don't have to look far to see someone who thought they had power and control until there was an accident, a downsizing at a company, or even a life-changing diagnosis. Chances are, you don't even need to look anywhere other than your own life to find a time when an external force changed an entire plan or outlook.

True power, as we'll discuss in later chapters, is not about holding on to external control. It's about the internal sense of agency: the ability to navigate life's challenges without dominating or manipulating every situation. You need to ensure you have the right compass to navigate this complicated world. External powers can alter any journey by leading you off course. Having the right compass will help get you back on track.

The more we chase the illusion of *permanent* power, the more we risk missing the true source of our strength: the balance between awareness of inner confidence and the acceptance that we cannot control everything. Internal and external power are often in conflict rather than in balance. Achieving balance is incredibly difficult but not impossible.

Finding Peace in Powerlessness

The paradox is this: sometimes, the more we accept the idea of *powerlessness*, the more we find real power. Chapter 4 ended with the phrase, *"Feeling powerless is not the same as being powerless."* This speaks to the opposing forces of external and internal power.

When those with external power make you *feel* powerless, you *have* the power to control how you act and choose to move forward. Finding peace in the absence of external power enables you to discover and cultivate your internal power.

Think of it like driving. You can't control the traffic lights, stop signs, or even how others drive. That powerlessness gives you the power to control your car. You get to determine how you will react to obstacles and hazards of the road. You have the power to hit the brakes or your horn. You have the power to speed up or slow down. You are *powerless* with respect to your external environment, but you are *powerful* in how you respond to it.

When we stop grasping for control and release the need to dominate, we begin to reconnect with what's truly important: ourselves, our relationships, our values, and our peace of mind. Letting go of the obsessive need to control everything can free us to be more present and authentic in every situation. This ability to connect and grow will give us the internal power we need to achieve the external power we desire.

In the next chapter, we will explore how the pursuit of power can lead to chaos and how understanding the balance of power can help restore harmony in our lives.

Reflection Questions

1. What forms of external power or validation do you find yourself chasing most often: status, approval, money, influence, recognition, or something else? Why do you think those things feel so important to you?
2. Think about a time when you achieved something you thought would finally make you feel secure, fulfilled, or powerful. How long did that feeling last, and what did that experience teach you?
3. What would it look like for you to measure power less by what you possess or achieve and more by how you respond, who you are becoming, and how aligned you are with your values?

CHAPTER 6

THE CHAOS OF THE POWER CHASE

The pursuit of power, when unchecked, creates chaos both within and around us.

The last chapter discussed the cyclical nature of chasing power and the chaos that ensues. It's a never-ending cycle: the more we pursue power, the more we feel the need for it. This pursuit comes at a high cost. There are various emotional costs involved, including stress, anxiety, burnout, and feelings of isolation.

In our current age of technology, we connect with millions of people across the globe through social media. The digital connection seems to have no impact on actual connection. In fact, studies are consistently showing people are feeling more disconnected and isolated than ever, leading to mental health concerns and even increased suicide rates.

This sounds like quite the paradox until you consider perception. Social media has become an arena where we change ourselves to impress others. Social media tends to highlight extremes and distort reality. People post the glamorous parts of life or intentionally seek out drama for attention. That could be why some of the most viral videos today are showing how these posts are fabricated. Focusing on the drama or idolizing those who embellish the good life of fame and fortune leaves us too afraid to share our reality with others.

This idea of only sharing things that get more likes, shares, and attention is similar to the chaos of the power chase. The more we engage in social media, the more inadequate we feel. With inadequacy comes fear, which prevents us from sharing aspects of our lives and having vulnerable conversations that lead to actual social connection.

Essentially, the more we chase social media, the less social we become. Like the façade of social media posts rooted in artificial intelligence and environmental manipulation to get the perfect shot, chasing power is an illusion of gaining something we are actually giving away. Just like with social media, the more we chase and think we gain external power, the less power we actually have.

We see this in everyday life, too, with products. Consider modern technology. Video games, computers, and smartphones all follow the same cycle because it works. Almost every year, a new smartphone comes out. Year to year, there are small differences between models, yet we know we need them.

One year, it's a little extra memory. We need that to store pictures and videos. The year after that, it's a slightly better camera. If we are storing pictures and videos, they must be of the highest quality. The following year brings more of the same: minor changes that have nothing to do with the device's overall functionality, originally intended for us to simply reach others with a simple call or text, regardless of where we are.

We rationalize each new feature as a need, and before we know it, we have rationalized ourselves into the cycle of the power chase. More memory, more processing speed, more applications, and now we are stuck relying on a device in our hand at all times to simply function throughout the day.

Look up from this book, and I would imagine it won't take long for you to see someone with their face looking down, buried in their phone screen. It is becoming commonplace to see someone so tethered to their smartphone that they sit on the floor next to a charging plug while they continue to scroll. Maybe you even see someone who seems to be talking to themselves; then you look closely and notice an earbud. Even worse, someone is walking down the hall on speakerphone for the entire world to hear their conversation.

This cycle goes back even further than modern smartphones. Before smartphones, we had phones that we could plug into our cars. Before that, there were payphones on many street corners. Keep going, and we communicated with phones in our house that had long cords because if we wanted to talk, we couldn't go very far. Even before that were telegrams and letters.

What began as a way to meet the real need to communicate faster and to improve safety, efficiency, and connection has now become an endless cycle of needing more. Now that smartphones enable us to order food, facilitate deliveries, navigate our travels, and connect us to others in an instant, anytime, anywhere, we can't even function for an entire day without these little devices.

What started as a way to meet a need turned into a chase for convenience and has come at a cost for control. Studies are linking technology use to attention and mood disorders, lack of critical thinking, and inability to connect with others. In essence, people are sacrificing control for the power of convenience. This is the same in life: the more we chase power, the more control we lose.

We've become so reliant on these smart devices that it feels like we're being controlled by them. We've always chased after the next best thing, and now we find ourselves in a situation where, without these devices, we struggle to keep up. Often, we lack a way to make money, engage with others, or engage with social media without them.

We see these devices as giving us the power to connect, influence, earn income, or simply capture moments. In reality, by chasing more memory, more functionality, and higher processing speeds, we have given up control to these devices.

At first, the chase for power might seem exhilarating. It's driven by ambition, desire, and the promise of control over our own destiny. But the deeper we go into this pursuit, the more we realize that power, like any external goal, comes with its own set of consequences. With power, the consequences are often paradoxical: the more we try to seize it, the more it slips through our fingers, leaving us feeling empty, disillusioned, and out of control. The more we gain, the more we lose. The illusion of power comes at the cost of actual control.

If you have ever been in a ball pit, you can relate to the struggle of chasing power. When you first dive in, it's a lot of fun. Once you try to get out, the struggle begins. Each step you take seems to make little progress. You try to get your footing, but the balls can't hold your weight. The more you climb, the more you sink. You must shimmy to the edge and use your arms (and sometimes help) to pull yourself out.

The power cycle is very similar. It's great when you first have power. Eventually, you will want to spend time in other areas of life (family, hobbies, etc.). Every time you try to focus on something else, the need for power pulls you back. It takes some work and often a little help to break the cycle.

The Destructive Cycle

The constant chase for power doesn't have a finish line. It's an infinite race, with no clear winner. Once we reach one goal, such as financial success, social influence, or professional status, we quickly set our sights on the next one. There's always something more to achieve, more to control, and more to conquer. There is always going to be someone ahead of you with more power and influence.

We see this a lot in today's society. The phrase "keeping up with the Joneses" is very real. We see others have something, and we must have it, too. We constantly chase the power of influence, aiming to have at least as much, if not more, than the next person. If my neighbor gets a new car, I need a Mercedes. If my coworker comes to work in brand-new clothes, I want an Armani suit.

Would it really matter if I drove a common car brand or an exotic one? Not really. Either car will take you where you want to go. When we buy the best brands, we have the best... for now. Next year brings a new car model, typically with little difference from what we already have. We still want it, though, because it sure would be nice to have a sunroof. In the end, we are left with two choices: buy the best brand and keep chasing power or keep the "dated" model and accept that what we have really does meet our needs.

This never-ending drive creates a cycle of *dissatisfaction*. Even when we achieve what we want, we still feel that something is missing. The feeling of power, once attained, is fleeting and ultimately unsatisfying. And so, we move on to the next goal, hoping that *this* time, power will bring us what we truly desire.

But power never delivers lasting happiness. It only creates a deeper craving for more. We become like a hamster on a wheel, constantly running but never reaching an end. The goals come around and around, but the wheel never stops.

Power and the Loss of Balance

When power becomes the central focus of our lives, it unbalances everything. Our relationships, our mental health, and our sense of self become casualties of our obsession with control. The more we chase control to fix our problems, the more out of balance we become. Our internal relationships, mental health, and self-worth are the keys to rebalancing ourselves, yet they are the very things we sacrifice to chase power.

By constantly chasing power, we begin to view everything and everyone through the lens of power dynamics. People become allies or obstacles; they either give power or take it away. Every interaction begins to be viewed through this lens. If we think someone can give us power, such as a new job, promotion, raise, or recommendation, we act as if we want to tap into their power for personal gain. If we see someone as inferior to us, having less money, status, or education, we begin to give them less time and attention.

Either result is manipulation. We are either manipulating ourselves or others. We are either changing our behavior to obtain what we perceive as power, or we are manipulating others to change their behavior to improve our perceived self-worth.

The Emotional Cost of Gaining Power

Power isn't just about having balance. What we perceive as power through external forces comes at a huge emotional cost. Chasing external power comes at the cost of relationships, which can lead to depression and isolation. External power brings titles and status, but at the cost of worrying about when it will all end. Money feels freeing until it runs out.

A few of the emotional costs include:

- **Stress and anxiety**: Constantly worrying about how to maintain what you have while also getting more. Worrying about when it will all be over because someone will take away that title and job, or the likes will start to slow down and shift to the next viral post.

- **Depression and isolation**: Alienating people in our lives by treating relationships as exchanges of power. Changing who we are and how we act based on what power we think others can offer us. Relationships become shallow, leaving us feeling more alone and disconnected. Over time, we can even lose sight of who we are as we constantly reshape ourselves to impress others.
- **Burnout, hopelessness, and despair**: The result of burning energy by constantly chasing power and a lack of meaningful relationships to recharge our need for connection. Being in the cycle for so long with no escape leads to advanced depression and higher suicide rates.

When in the midst of the chaos of the pursuit of power, we can easily and quickly lose focus on what really matters. Without connection and relationships, we lose the ability to thrive or even simply survive. By chasing external sources of power, such as success, recognition, control, status, and titles, we end up treating relationships as transactional. In the end, the emotional toll is much greater than the perceived power we achieve.

The False Perception of Control

One of the most attractive aspects of power is control. Unfortunately, no matter how much we think power equals control, it rarely does. Control is more of an illusion than reality, at least when it comes to external forces. We can wish, plan, and predict all we want, but ultimately the results are rarely within our control.

We can control how we travel to work (walk, drive, or take public transportation), but we can't control someone who isn't paying attention and causes an accident. We can go to work and focus on our task at hand, but we usually lack control over a company that decides to sell, downsize, or eliminate the job we do. We can save up money, but we can't predict when a storm will blow through, causing us to spend it on repairs.

We often think power equals control, but in reality, there is very little we can control. In the end, the power chase creates a cycle where we give up the very power and control we are chasing.

The power cycle uses the illusion of control to control you. Power becomes an addiction. The more you have, the more you need. The more you strive for power, the more you lose in life. We chase power to gain control, yet we often lose control to gain power.

Some say money equals power. That is a great illustration. The more money people get, the more they tend to spend. The more they spend, the more they need. In the end, power controls us by the need to constantly have more.

The desire to achieve power and control can make us rigid and inflexible. Focusing on such a goal requires sacrifices. Time, money, and relationships are all casualties of the pursuit of power. We become so focused on obtaining the goal that we stop at nothing to achieve it.

Staying on task requires a certain amount of rigidity in the form of discipline, but we must be able to adapt along the journey to obstacles in the path. If we are constantly rigid and inflexible, we lack the ability to adapt to change, which keeps us from staying on course. Life doesn't go according to plan.

Being too rigid prevents us from realizing this and being ready for changes to the plan. Feeling out of control and powerless can feel overwhelming.

Rebalancing

The key to escaping the chaos of the power chase is balance. A balanced approach comes from a balanced view. Instead of viewing external forces as something to control, recognize that the only control we have is over our own actions and responses.

We control our mindset. We have the choice to pick which pair of perceptual glasses we use to look at the world, which lens we will use to see things around us. We can't control when it will rain, but we can control if we bring an umbrella, get mad when we step into a puddle, or stop and dance in the rain. We can recognize that power is not the ability to control the world but our response to it.

True power isn't in conquering the outer world; it comes from mastering the inner world. Power comes when we are able to refocus the lens of our perceptions. It comes from enjoying the world and interacting with it, from building relationships. Trying to control the rain isn't powerful. Stopping to splash in the puddle and dance in the rain is. Trying to control other people isn't powerful. Creating meaningful connections with them is. Power isn't something that is gained; it's something we already have.

Changing our perception will allow us to let go of the obsession to pursue external power. Getting out of the cycle of the power chase provides freedom. Without being preoccupied with the power chase, we are free to choose how we see the world and how we react to it.

Even better, taking a new perspective doesn't just stop the power cycle. Choosing to look for another view puts us in a cycle of growth rather than one of destruction. The more we look for different perspectives, the more we find them. The more we discover them, the more we keep looking.

With a different understanding, we can empathize and connect with each other. When we keep stepping back to learn more, we step away from the power chase.

In the next chapter, we will continue to explore the intersection of power and perception. We will dive into how our responses to the world around us lead to influence, which is true external power.

Reflection Questions

1. Where in your life do you notice yourself caught in a cycle of "more": more success, more recognition, more possessions, or more control? How does that pursuit affect your sense of balance?
2. Think about a time when chasing an external goal or form of power created stress, anxiety, or imbalance in your life. What did that experience teach you about what truly matters?
3. What is one small step you could take to shift from chasing external power to strengthening your internal balance, relationships, or sense of purpose?

CHAPTER 7

HOW PERCEPTION LEADS TO BEHAVIOR

How we perceive leads to how we behave.

Perception isn't just about view; it's about behavior. How we see things determines how we respond. If we feel unsafe or threatened, we will do anything to ensure safety, even if it seems irrational. The same is true when we focus more on perceived power rather than on how we view things.

Perception serves as a blueprint for our actions; it shapes how we interpret our environment and dictates our reactions to those interpretations. Our interpretation of the environment is most often through the lens shaped by our different beliefs, views, biases, education, and life experiences.

Now we will examine how these perceptions affect not only our physical responses but also our emotional ones.

You've already learned that perception shapes the lens through which we view events, people, and situations. But perception isn't just a passive experience. It's an active force that drives our actions. The way we interpret our environment guides our responses, our decisions, and even our interactions with others. If perception is the way we filter reality, then behavior is the *outward expression* of that filtered reality. It is the end result of how the world was filtered.

Think about your morning coffee. The beans are bitter, so why is coffee so popular? Why are there so many different flavors and ways to make it? The beans are filtered by how they are roasted, the device used to run water through the coffee grounds, the water-to-coffee ratio, and even the additions at the end (sugar, creamer, etc.). The world provides the beans, and our experiences provide the sugar and creamer. The flavor we created is our outward expression. This is also true because each cup is different, just like each expression is different.

Perception as the Blueprint for Action

Imagine you're walking down the street when someone approaches you, looking a bit disheveled and asking for help. How you respond to this situation depends entirely on how you *perceive* it.

- If you perceive the person as genuinely in need, you might stop offering assistance because you feel empathy and compassion.
- If you perceive the person as a potential threat or manipulator, you might cross the street, avoid eye contact, or keep walking.
- If you are distracted or used to encountering people fitting this description, you may not respond at all.

If the situation is the same, why is the response different? Because people differ in their perceptions of life. Those who have experienced homelessness might be more empathetic and willing to help. Someone with a view of homelessness as a direct result of poor choices and addiction might look at but intentionally avoid the person. Anyone who sees many people like this on their daily commute is likely more inclined to simply tune the situation out and remain oblivious to it.

This situation resonates throughout life. Whether deciding how to approach a new project, having or avoiding difficult conversations, or handling a setback, your perception of the situation controls your response. A new project can be well-structured or incredibly fluid. Dealing with a situation through conversation rather than avoidance depends on how you have handled it in the past. A sudden change in course can be devastating or a chance for an extraordinary new adventure. The choice is yours.

The Power of Interpretation

We started this book with the idea that our reality isn't *the* reality. The same is true with perception. Our perception isn't always *the* perception; it's shaped by the lens of our own life. Someone else will have a completely different perception of the same situation because they are viewing it through a different lens.

This also explains why there is so much division in society. Societies can't seem to agree on human rights, immigration, economics, or any other aspect because everyone sees things through a different lens, leading to different beliefs about what's best.

Human rights remain a major issue across the globe. Countries are still at war and in political conflict over various human rights issues. If they are "rights," why is there disagreement? Because different perspectives offer different ideas of what rights are and what is right. Differences in attitudes toward topics such as who we can marry and how we treat others are a direct result of differing perspectives.

Take a look at popular culture, such as movies, shows, music, and fashion, and you will see this in action. My favorite is reading movie critics' reviews. So many movies often receive bad reviews yet are popular after release. The reason is that the critics are watching the movie through a different lens than everyone else. A critic is looking at the lighting, the background acting, the music, the script, and every little detail. When people go to a movie, they just want to be entertained. This even spills over into awards shows. The movies awarded by industry professionals always seem to differ from those chosen by the public.

The Lens of Bias

Bias, at its simplest, is the direction toward which we tend to gravitate. If we have a sweet tooth, we may gravitate toward desserts whenever we pass them. A sports enthusiast will gravitate toward the game. When looking for relationships, we gravitate toward people more like us.

Bias is natural and not necessarily as bad as it sounds. These gravitations are generally designed to help us make decisions without even thinking about it. The issue with bias is that it is deeply ingrained. When left unchecked, it becomes not just what dessert to eat but how we judge the people and things around us. While bias comes in many forms, a few examples include:

- **Confirmation**: Gravitating toward supporting what we already know or believe. Only reading information from sources that share our opinions is a great example of this. Another is social media algorithms: after a few similar clicks, they will start filling your feed with content similar to what you looked at.
- **Anchoring**: Relying on the first piece of information you see or hear. Just because it was the first thing you read doesn't mean it was the most accurate. Also, information changes over time. It is important to confirm information before spreading it. The recent pandemic was a

great reminder of this. Research changed information. If everyone had simply gone with the first thing they read about the disease, we might not have eventually returned to normal.

- **Availability**: Treating our reality as *the* reality. With this, we tend to react based on our limited experience rather than overall data or numbers.
- **Framing**: Intentionally presenting information in a way to get a response. This is a clear example of our perception leading to interpretation. To see this, pretend you are sick. You have a 50 percent chance of recovery. How was this information presented to you? Do you have a 50 percent chance to live or a 50 percent chance to die?
- **First impression**: Forming an entire opinion about someone based on your first meeting. The problem here is that the impression is often based on physical appearance rather than deeper meaning. This bias, for example, can lead us to believe that people are good or bad based on their appearance. Someone well put together is viewed as competent and capable, while someone unkempt is not.

Eliminating biases is an impossible task. The goal is to recognize them so you can be aware of and understand how they shape your interactions with the world around you. When you are aware of your bias, you can step back and see if you are forming a picture based on good or bad tendencies.

If unchecked, our biases can exert control over our lives. We focus on biased sources that support our views rather than simply present factual information, judge people we have never met based solely on their looks, and develop habits of comfort that will eventually stunt our personal growth.

Perception's Influence on Emotions and Responses

Our perceptions also influence our emotions. If we perceive an event as threatening, we are likely to feel fear, anxiety, or anger. If we perceive it as an opportunity, we may feel excitement, motivation, or joy.

Perception influences our reactions on both conscious and unconscious levels. At the unconscious level, we often make quick decisions based on our instincts. For instance, when you perform a familiar task you do every day, you don't need to research it; you rely on your past experience, which tells you it's fine to proceed in a certain way. Thus, these decisions are made rapidly and unconsciously, which can be beneficial for navigating through daily life, such as choosing where to eat.

On a physical level, consider what happens when you're driving and approach a traffic light. Imagine you're simply driving along when the light turns from green to yellow. At this moment, your perception of the situation will guide your next actions without the need for extensive thought about external factors, like being late for work. What do you do when the light turns yellow? Do you step on the gas to speed up and try to make it through, or do you slow down and prepare to stop because you know it's going to turn red?

Your perception and experiences will significantly influence your behavior in this situation. For example, someone involved in a T-bone accident is likely to learn from that experience. They will probably be the type of person who hits the brakes when the light turns yellow, wanting to ensure they stop, either because they are wary of reliving that incident or simply want to avoid a similar situation in the future.

On the other hand, people who choose to speed up and make it through the yellow light may not have faced any repercussions before, or may simply have grown up in an area where traffic lights were treated as mere suggestions. They might have never been in an accident or received a ticket. If they've successfully made it through before, they could easily feel confident doing so again.

These varying experiences will shape how people react when they see that light turn yellow. Will they hit the brakes and stop, or will they hit the gas and drive through, assuming everything will be fine?

Think about your response to this scenario. Emotions drive our behavior. Fear can cause us to avoid challenges or take defensive actions. Excitement can push us to take risks or try something new. For example, if you perceive a challenging situation as a potential learning opportunity, you might approach it with a growth mindset, leading you to take proactive steps and persist in the face of difficulty.

However, if you perceive the same situation as an insurmountable obstacle, you might withdraw or give up before trying. This is often seen in motivational success stories. The people who reached their goals persisted against all odds because they viewed obstacles as opportunities and were not deterred.

The Self-Fulfilling Prophecy

Perception also plays a key role in what psychologists call the *self-fulfilling prophecy*: the idea that what we expect often becomes true simply because we believe it will. If you perceive yourself as someone who always fails at new challenges, you may avoid taking risks, thus reinforcing your belief. On the other hand, if you believe you can succeed, your behavior will likely be bolder, more strategic, and more persistent, increasing your chances of success.

This unconscious decision-making can lead to negative outcomes that foster fear and anxiety. For example, when we're overly worried about an impending meeting with our boss, we might fear the worst: that we're not performing well, that we'll receive harsh criticism, or even that we might lose our job or face a pay cut. These fears can cloud our judgment, leading us to behave in ways that inadvertently create the negative scenarios we dread.

This is the power of perception: it can create a cycle that either propels us forward or holds us back. What we believe about ourselves, others, and the world often becomes our reality. More often than we realize, the results we receive are due to our doubts and fears working subconsciously to guide our decisions to the result we didn't want but just *knew* would happen.

I see this most often in children. Two children can have different results on the monkey bars, not because of physical differences, but because of perceptual ones. One child is sure they won't make it to the other side. Though their parents encourage and cheer them on, when they try, they likely fail. Why? Because they knew they would. The next kid comes up, certain that they can do anything, and flies across to the other side. Why? Because they knew they would. Each fulfilled their own prophecy.

We can either fail because we just know we will, or we can take time to learn why we feel that way and overcome the obstacles that make us feel defeated before it even comes.

Controlling Perception to Make Exercise the Power of Choice

So many aspects of our lives shape our perceptions. We have already talked about how the various things that make us unique are the same ones that give us our unique lens of perspective. Controlling our perceptions is the key to unlocking the true power: the power of choice.

When we consciously think about how we interpret information and look for different angles, we effectively give ourselves the power to choose how we respond. Taking control of our perceptions gives us control over our behavior. Being aware that we have tendencies to gravitate toward certain feelings and actions allows us to pause, giving us the freedom to choose how we respond.

Here's an example of that in action. I was at a movie theater, watching a movie I had been wanting to see for some time. If you have gone to a movie recently, you know it isn't cheap. I sat down and got comfortable. A few minutes after the movie started (not the previews, the actual movie), a large group came in and sat behind me: two adults and several kids. This movie was not for small children, yet several were sitting behind me, and the entire group was making quite a bit of noise.

After a few opening scenes, the adults decided to move down to my row, walking in front of me to get to the end. For the rest of the movie, they talked back and forth while loosely supervising children who shouldn't have been there in the first place. One toddler was having a hard time sitting still and being quiet, and one of the adults would walk in front of me twice whenever there was an issue: once to get to the kid and once to get back to their seat.

At first, I wanted to get mad. I'd paid a lot of money for this movie, and I certainly hadn't paid for this distraction. Eventually, I started to notice something that changed my perspective a bit. While the actions could be considered very rude, the adults apologized almost every time they walked in front of me. They even ducked as they walked past, trying not to block the screen.

It finally dawned on me that this was a couple doing the best they could. The kids were of different ages. I would imagine the toddler was there because they were trying to take the older child to a movie he had wanted to see and didn't have anyone to watch the toddler. They likely moved down after getting the children situated because they rarely got any time alone. I am sure most parents can relate.

While the distractions were a bit inconvenient, I paused to look at the bigger picture. I was able to control my actions (take a breath and adapt rather than complain to the theater management or berate the couple in front of their children) and enjoy the rest of the movie.

Such pauses are powerful. We will talk more about that later, but it can't happen without self-awareness of our internal biases and the intentional seeking out of new information and perspectives to change our own.

Unconscious biases are useful for forming quick opinions when there isn't much time to decide. They're great for deciding where to eat and what to wear. However, these internal biases make us react without getting the whole story. Being aware of these internal biases is foundational to taking a step back and gathering more information. More information means more choices. We can choose to be guided by quick, subconscious decisions, or we can pause to learn, grow, and make conscious ones.

Unchecked biases lead to making choices based on emotion and partial truths. Having conscious awareness of bias allows us to gather more information and rely more on logic when making a choice. This shift from an emotional to a logical mindset creates an opportunity to choose our responses. We can choose to quickly judge and disconnect ourselves from others, or we can choose to be empathetic and grow in connection.

Next, we will build on the ideas of power and perception by examining how they interact. We will also look at how to balance them and how achieving this gives us power.

Reflection Questions

1. Can you identify a time when your interpretation of a situation later turned out to be incomplete or incorrect? What changed your understanding?
2. How might pausing to question your interpretation of a situation change the way you respond to challenges, conflicts, or misunderstandings?
3. What is one area of your life where becoming more aware of your perceptions could help you make more intentional choices about your behavior?

CHAPTER 8

THE POWER AND PERCEPTION BALANCE

Power and perception are two forces that shape every aspect of our lives.

Achieving a balance between them is essential. We have learned that perception is the lens through which we view the world; it's how we understand power. We've defined power and discussed how many people equate it with authority.

However, true power encompasses much more than that. It involves integrating these concepts to establish a balance that allows us to regain some control over our situations.

Earlier, we touched on the concepts of illusion and control. The goal now is to better understand and manage that control and achieve a balance that can help shift your perception. Maintaining this balance is crucial.

As we discussed, power isn't merely about having authority. Real power lies in how you influence the world around you. Recognizing that you possess this form of power empowers you to take a moment to reflect, engage in meaningful conversations, develop relationships, evaluate your perceptions, and make more deliberate decisions, ultimately helping you maintain equilibrium.

While power and perception are interconnected, they must be kept in balance to avoid the pitfalls of overreach, insecurity, or disconnection. When the balance is right, power can be a force for good, allowing us to navigate the world with confidence, authenticity, and impact. When they are out of balance, we risk emotionally charged responses and snap decisions driven by bias, misinformation, and misjudgment.

Understanding how power and perception work together and how to balance them is the key to unlocking the ability to choose. As mentioned in the previous chapter, choice brings power. The power of choice will not only keep these two forces in balance but also allow you to harness their full potential.

Perception as the Energy Source of Power

How we define power will determine how we use it. How we perceive it will determine whether we are stuck in the chase for superficial power or can take a step back and start gaining real power.

If we see power as finite, something to be taken or hoarded, we may approach it with a scarcity mindset. We see it as something we must gain by taking away from others. This mindset causes damage and destruction. Externally, it alienates others and turns everyday interactions into transactions based on who can either offer you power or take it away. Internally, titles and status provide a false sense of security that ultimately undermines genuine authority.

On the other hand, if we shift our perception of power to see it as an abundant, renewable energy source, we can gain the very thing promised but never achieved in the power chase. Realizing power is about self-awareness, and pausing to gain different perspectives before making a choice leads to growth, collaboration, understanding, success, and impact in the world around you.

Being able to relate to and understand someone fosters connection, leading to stronger relationships that can overcome the destruction caused by the power chase. When we build relationships, we not only gain more power but are also renewed through growth and connection.

Think about championship sports teams. What do they have in common? I am sure most people immediately think of superstars and Hall of Fame players. However, several Hall of Famers have never won a championship. Why? Because it takes more than one player. Teams win championships because of every player on the team.

This is also true in industry. A company can have the best person at the top running the entire organization. Without people to carry out their vision, the company wouldn't be successful. Take Amazon, for example. While Jeff Bezos may have had the vision and started the company from the ground up, it couldn't operate at its current size without everyone's help. No drivers means no delivery. No tech support means no app. No products means nothing to sell. No customer service means no customers. To be the best at anything means having the best team working toward the same goal.

The Role of Perception in Wielding Power

The way we perceive our power can determine how we wield it. When we perceive ourselves as powerful, we act with confidence and clarity. But when our perception of our power is skewed by doubt or insecurity, we may hesitate, overcompensate, or act in ways that undermine our authority.

For example, someone who perceives themselves as a strong leader may naturally take charge in a situation, guiding others with clarity and vision. However, someone who feels insecure in their leadership abilities might struggle to make decisions, second-guess themselves, or adopt a defensive posture. In either case, their behavior is shaped by their perception of their power.

Likewise, how we perceive others' power affects how we interact with them. If we see someone as more powerful than we are, whether because of their position, expertise, or charisma, we may defer to them or, conversely, feel threatened and resistant. But if we perceive someone's power as complementary to our own, we're more likely to collaborate and form a productive partnership.

Of course, the third option is for us to demand submission of others based on the power we perceive we have. If you are under the impression that people are beneath you because of your perceived power, you may need a different book.

Consider how we react in everyday conflicts. This is where we start to see the practical application of these ideas. For example, a loved one, such as your best friend, a family member, your spouse, or your child, approaches you and asks, "Why didn't you take out the trash?" How will you respond? Will you immediately reply, "I've been a little busy. I'll get to it"?

Compare that to a similar situation at work. With family or friends, you might feel more comfortable making quick judgments and expressing yourself candidly. You may not feel as judged for your biases, or perhaps you've surrounded yourself with people who share them. Consequently, these dynamics often go unrecognized because they are shaped by your upbringing and environment. You chose your spouse, and you're the one raising your child. There are many similarities in these roles, and there's comfort in that.

However, when you go to work and your boss asks, "Why didn't you get this project done on time?" You don't snap back. You don't say, "I had to answer a phone call for thirty minutes."

If you are more passive, you may say nothing and reach out to someone you trust to lend a listening ear to make you feel better. If you are more assertive, you are likely to research to validate your thoughts and then express them professionally to your boss. I am sure the response is well composed and eloquently stated. Either way, you take a breath, stay calm, apologize, and make adjustments to get the work done.

This illustrates the balance we must find in our reactions. Your power lies in how you respond, not in your authority. Your influence in a situation with your boss doesn't stem from their authority over you; it comes from your ability to control your reactions. How you respond to your friends and family will determine if you will create a cycle of dysfunction or break it.

Ultimately, our experiences shape how we respond to situations. Understanding this can help us navigate our reactions more effectively.

Power and the Balance of Influence

True power lies not in dominance or control but in the ability to control our choices and, in turn, influence and inspire others. To maintain a healthy balance between power and perception, we must learn to use our influence responsibly. This means being mindful of how we affect others and ensuring that our actions align with our values.

We see this dynamic a lot on social media, especially in many viral videos. I can recall a time before social media when television programs would feature funny videos. One that stands out is of a little boy playing golf. He hits the ball well, and his mother, who is filming, encourages him to show how his dad does it. After hitting the ball hard, the boy hurls away his golf club and throws a small fit, imitating his father's behavior.

A more recent viral video is the "Listen, Linda" video. In this clip, a toddler is frustrated with his mother and repeatedly insists, "Linda, listen!" We laugh at this because it's amusing to see such earnestness from a young child. But it raises an important question: where did he learn to speak to his mother like that? He learned it from his environment and experience, by witnessing how others interact with his mother.

Similarly, the young golfer threw his club because he had observed his dad reacting that way when he didn't make a shot he liked. We continue to mimic the behaviors of others based on who we allow to influence our lives. The fact that "influencer" is now an actual career speaks volumes to how we still seek validation by imitating others.

A balanced approach to power is rooted in empathy and awareness. These two characteristics recognize that power is not something to be hoarded but something to be shared, cultivated, and used to elevate others. Being self-aware is the foundational first step and must be followed by empathy.

It is important to recognize that we interpret information through our own lens. While we are coming to one conclusion, others have created their own. This creates many possibilities for problem-solving. How we interpret and accept information will determine our actions. Our actions will determine how effectively we lead, influence, and create change.

Perhaps the most important part of this is that balance doesn't take power away; it gives it in abundance. By exercising the power to seek out someone else's perspective, we gain the power to connect. Through connection, we gain the power to lead, influence, and create change. Power isn't something that is found and hoarded away; it is something that is gained by giving.

Allowing others to be open and honest without judgment gives them the power to have a voice. Listening without judgment creates the power of connection. Through connection, change, and growth can occur. When this happens, people can even have respectful disagreements that allow harmony and combat destruction.

Balancing perception and power creates opportunities to be heard, to express feelings, to build trust, and to cultivate growth.

Power Without Perception

We have already talked about the dangers of power alone, but it is worth reiterating. Power without the right perception is harmful. Power alone seeks various forms of domination, exploitation, and authoritative control. Wielding power without perception, understanding, and empathy causes damage. Often, the damage caused by seeking power without the right perception is irreversible and catastrophic.

Take, for example, a company leader: a manager, director, vice president, or president. A leader who uses their power to manipulate or control others for personal gain may alienate those around them, leaving them isolated and full of mistrust. Not listening to and showing empathy for those doing the work leads to decreased efficiency, employee burnout, and resignations, resulting in costly turnover.

A leader who is empathetic and listens to their employees creates an environment that is more efficient and has lower operating costs. Surveys consistently show that employees are willing to stay even if pay is lower, as long as their leader and the company treat them well.

When power and perception are unbalanced, power becomes a force that undermines rather than supports, and it divides rather than unites. It creates environments where people feel unseen, unheard, and unvalued. Without perception, power tips the balance toward chaos and destruction. It can alienate and divide people.

True power lies in our ability to pause and reflect. Power is the ability to gather more information and understanding and to connect. It's important to understand that our strength comes from how we respond to situations, rather than from what we have authority over.

Perception Without Power

On the flip side, perception without power can also be problematic. When we perceive ourselves as lacking power or influence, we may act passively, avoid challenges, or fail to take initiative or risks. This leads to missed opportunities and a reinforced sense of powerlessness. When we are so preoccupied with finding everyone else's perception, we are unable to identify our own.

Perception without power can also cause us to underestimate our abilities, shrink in the face of adversity, or hold back our potential because we are unsure of who we are or what we feel. I am sure you can imagine a time when you didn't pursue something simply because you thought you weren't good enough. Your perception may have kept you from experiencing growth or adventure.

The person who believes they have no power might fail to speak up in meetings, avoid taking on leadership roles, or refrain from standing up for their beliefs. They may also allow others to dominate conversations or decisions, not realizing that their voice and actions are just as valuable.

Feeling powerless also prevents us from speaking up and advocating for others. Sound familiar? Chances are, you can see where you have done this once or twice in your life. I am sure there was a time you saw someone being mistreated but stayed silent because it wasn't your issue. And this hesitation doesn't just apply to how we mistreat others but also to how we sometimes mistreat ourselves. Almost all of us have had a time when we were being criticized and didn't speak up.

Perception without power creates its own dangerous cycle. In this instance, feeling powerless and having self-doubt leads to inaction. Being paralyzed by these negative beliefs leads to even more inaction. Pretty soon, the cycle leaves you in a constant state of retreat and prevents you from forming meaningful relationships where you are seen and heard. Without relationships, the cycle just continues, leaving you unable to exert influence or effect change.

The power you have over your thoughts and actions is far greater than any power you may think you have over other people or events. You always have the power to control what you think, say, and do. As we mentioned earlier, this will control the influence you have on those around you.

Self-Reflecting to Achieve Balance

Achieving balance between power and perception requires self-reflection. This process brings to light the lens you use to view the world around you and shows how your actions are based on your views.

Self-reflection requires the ability to intentionally seek out your biases and be open to listening to others. Openness allows you to check your own views with those of others to find a balance. It is easy to be a self-critic, but we need other perspectives to gain an accurate perspective of ourselves.

For example, maybe you talk a lot. Self-criticism sees this through the lens of being frequently in trouble for talking too much or simply wanting to be more like "normal" people who don't get into trouble for talking. From the outside, this same characteristic of talking a lot may actually be a trait of success. Often, the same kids who "talk too much in school" are the adults who can make connections with others.

Self-reflection is the ability to get feedback from the world around you to gain a balanced view. If you were a kid who talked too much, I bet this same attribute has given you meaningful relationships and opened up opportunities for growth. It may even be the same reason you are successful in your career.

Moving from self-criticism to self-reflection requires looking not just at your own view but also at others' perspectives. Balancing your perception requires:

- **Self-awareness**: Internal reflection on how you view yourself and the world around you. Understanding what shapes the lens you use to view things and how it leads to your actions. Moving from unintentional responses to intentional behaviors.
- **External feedback**: Actively seeking feedback from outside sources. Gathering more information to compare perspectives.
- **Connection**: Creating relationships and connections to use feedback as growth. Empathetic listening builds relationships, helping you gain feedback and find a partner for growth.
- **Adaptability**: Responding to the feedback. This can come in the form of change or not. Either way, it is growth. By making connections, listening empathetically, and being open to feedback, you may feel you need to make some adjustments. While that is obviously growth, finding validation that supports not changing builds self-confidence, which is growth, too.

Balancing power and perception creates harmony that leads to both internal and external growth. Internally, balance leads to integrity, self-awareness, self-acceptance, and self-confidence. Externally, the balance allows for empathy and connection.

Real change comes through meaningful relationships. Relationships provide feedback for growth, connection, influence, and collaboration. True power lies not in control, but in empowering others.

Once you begin to balance power and perception, you start to recognize the power you have to control your choices. The next chapter explores this idea further and shows how it leads to the realization of true power.

Reflection Questions

1. In your life right now, do you tend to lean more toward power without perception (control, authority, certainty) or perception without power (doubt, hesitation, passivity)? What might balance look like for you (listening more carefully, pausing before reacting, seeking feedback, or adjusting your response to a situation)?
2. Think about a recent interaction where your response was shaped by how powerful or powerless you felt. How might a different perception of your influence have changed your response?
3. How do you typically perceive the power of others? Do you see it as something that competes with your own power or something that can complement and strengthen it?

CHAPTER 9

REALIZATION OF POWER

Power isn't a commodity that is obtained and used; it is an internal, renewable force.

True power isn't about external forces or having authoritative control over something. True power lies in recognizing how we view the world and the possibility that there are different ways to look at something.

It's important to realize this definition of power. As previously discussed, the power chase is full of chaos and destruction. Control over anything external is fleeting and elusive. True power is about controlling our actions in various situations and the ability to make choices.

I should point out that making a choice doesn't always feel empowering, especially if we don't like the options available. However, the key takeaway is that we still possess the power to make a choice in every situation.

We discussed responding to feedback in the last chapter, whether it's negative comments from family, criticism at work, compliments on our recent weight loss, or kudos for a great job. No matter the environment, we can choose how we respond.

This discussion emphasizes the importance of self-awareness. Being self-aware allows us to overcome limiting beliefs. Going back to the example of my oldest daughter, she has struggled with the belief that she cannot accomplish certain things, and helping her overcome that mindset is an ongoing process. Her power lies in her ability to choose to try.

Realizing your power is the first step in taking control of your life, shaping your reality, and making meaningful changes in the world around you. Whether you feel powerful or powerless, it doesn't change the truth: you always have power over your actions and choices. What you do with that power and how you think, feel, and act will determine the influence you have on people and the world around you.

But how do we come to realize the power we already possess? Making the transition from powerless to powerful is difficult when you feel you have no control. This is why having a different view on the definition of power is so important.

This chapter will discuss how you have control, whether you think so or not. Accepting the idea that power is internal is the first step toward realizing that it has been within you all along.

Waking Internal (True) Power

Waking internal power starts with recognizing how we view the world and accepting different opinions. This leads to the realization that we are already powerful. Rather than seeking power and control externally, we need to look internally. External validation breeds dependence, but internal self-acceptance leads to confidence and endurance. The quest for external sources, such as money, status, and titles, takes power away, while embarking on the internal journey of self-realization gives power. It all starts with mindset and perspective.

True power isn't external. It comes from within. True power comes with realizing that at any moment, you have the ability to pause, intentionally interpret, and respond to information. You can always look for a different angle when stuck on something.

You can gather as much information as you would like before making a decision. When someone says something you don't like, you can always choose to decide if you will interpret that as hurtful and personal or if you will assume they are just trying to help you.

Recognizing your inherent power starts with understanding that you have control over your thoughts, actions, and responses. No matter your external circumstances, you have the ability to choose how you react and how you shape your reality. This is the essence of personal power: the ability to direct your energy, thoughts, and actions toward creating the life you want.

The best part? Taking power over yourself is how you control the power others have over you. That person who is always mean? There is a reason people say, "Kill them with kindness." The mean person expects you to react and fight back. You have the power to get mad and badmouth them or simply smile through it all.

The Power of Choice

The most powerful tool you have is choice. Every moment offers an opportunity to choose how you respond to a situation, how you interact with others, and how you direct your energy. The more you recognize that you always have a choice, the more empowered you will feel. There is always a choice. Admittedly, you may not always like either choice, but you always have one.

In difficult situations, this might mean choosing to stay calm and composed rather than reacting out of anger or fear. In relationships, it might mean choosing to listen with empathy rather than judging or criticizing. In moments of challenge, it might mean choosing to persevere rather than giving up. It could be choosing to ride the bus or drive a car to work, or deciding to spend your paycheck on bills or having fun, but there is always a choice. The key is being aware that you have the choice.

One of the best examples of this is the movie *The Matrix*. This famous movie franchise began as a blockbuster film and has led to a trilogy and a recent revival. In *The Matrix*, the main character, Neo, lives as a computer hacker. While he enjoys his everyday life of partying and working, something feels off. Eventually, he starts receiving strange messages that lead him to Morpheus, whom he initially believes is just another hacker.

As events unfold, Neo finds himself pursued by mysterious forces. This culminates in a pivotal scene in which he sits in a run-down building with Morpheus, who presents him with a choice: a blue pill or a red pill. If he takes the blue pill, he will forget their meeting and return to his mundane life. The red pill, however, will offer a new perspective he never could have imagined on his own.

In that moment, Neo faces a decision that will determine the direction of the rest of his life: he can return to his computer hacking, friends, parties, and everything else he enjoys, or leave this world to embark on an adventure that is completely different. No promise of the future, no other information, just two pills, two possibilities, and one choice.

The same is true in life. We always have the power of choice, and the consequences will impact our lives. The choice may not seem appealing. We may not like the options. We may not like the outcomes. We may not have all the information we want, but we always have a choice.

Many might even wonder how to return to their previous life or "undo" their choice if the outcome proves unpleasant. The reality is that experiencing something new is where true power lies: the power of choice.

Each time you make a conscious choice, you exercise your personal power. The more you make empowered choices, the more you begin to realize just how much influence you truly have over your life. It may sound cliché, but you truly can choose to be happy and embrace the world around you, or you can choose to feel powerless. Embracing your power of choice and choosing to influence your life is a lot like exercising. It is difficult at first, but once you get into the routine, you feel better every day.

Overcoming Limiting Beliefs

One of the greatest barriers to realizing our power is the limiting beliefs we hold about ourselves. These are the stories we tell ourselves about what we can and cannot do, about who we are and who we're not.

How many times have you kept yourself from trying because you "weren't good enough" to do it? Limiting beliefs are often born from past experiences, societal conditioning, or negative feedback we've received over time. We discussed past experiences earlier in this book. Understanding what makes you "you" will give you the power to be the "you" you want to be.

These beliefs can be deeply ingrained, but they are not permanent. Realize that your power often requires you to challenge and dismantle these limiting beliefs. When we begin to question the stories we've been telling ourselves, or the stories others have told us about ourselves, we open up space for new possibilities. We start to see that the limitations we once thought were real are, in fact, just perceptions that can be shifted.

By reframing the way we think about ourselves, we can tap into a new level of power. Instead of believing that we are too weak, too inexperienced, or too powerless to make a difference, we can choose to see ourselves as capable, resilient, and deserving of success. Ever text the wrong person? You can either let it bring you down or own it by laughing and learning from it.

The Power of Self-Awareness

Self-awareness is a key component of realizing your power. The more aware you are of your thoughts, emotions, and behaviors, the more control you have over them. Self-awareness allows you to see where you are giving away your power and where you are holding on to it. Self-awareness allows you to look at the things you have let control you and take power over them.

Developing self-awareness will also help you build confidence and foster a growth mindset. It's crucial to adopt the perspective that we must continually grow. If you look back and find that you are the same person today as you were ten years ago, it may indicate that you are not using your power to make choices effectively. We ought to evolve and learn from our experiences.

For example, if you are constantly seeking validation from others, you may be giving away your power. If you find yourself repeatedly in situations where you feel disempowered or controlled by others, it's important to examine how your perception of yourself and your power might be contributing to these patterns. Constantly seeking validation from others may stem from not receiving a lot of validation in your childhood. The antidote is confidence and self-validation.

Becoming aware of these dynamics and how you have been shaped by your past enables you to make conscious decisions about how to regain control. This starts with being aware of your past and accepting it as the basis for how you interact with the present. This leads to self-validation and self-confidence. Having awareness and confidence allows you to set the boundaries necessary to openly listen to new information and determine whether it aligns with your values and goals.

Having a Powerful Mindset

Having the right mindset is critical to accessing your power. Being fixed on one way of thinking limits your ability to gather new information and grow. Recognizing and accepting that things can change fosters a growth mindset. This allows for new perspectives, skills, and ideas.

A growth mindset creates new possibilities and learning. Being able to grow, develop, and learn allows you to challenge your perception and gauge its accuracy. Growth is often seen as change. However, being able to openly gain new understandings to validate your perceptions on life is still growth; it is growth in self. The more you challenge yourself, the stronger you get. The same is true with your beliefs and values. Challenging them and finding validation makes them stronger.

On the other hand, a fixed mindset, believing that your abilities are set in stone and that you are either capable or not, can lead to feelings of helplessness and stagnation. You may avoid risks or shy away from opportunities because you feel that your power is limited.

Remember, you always have the power to choose. Just because you have always chosen option A, it doesn't mean it is impossible for you to finally choose option B. Before long, one altered choice becomes another. Who knows? You may even feel like a whole new person! Our perceptions should shift as we gain new experiences and build relationships with the world around us.

To truly realize your power, you must adopt a growth mindset. This means seeing challenges as opportunities, setbacks as lessons, and progress as a continuous journey rather than a destination. If you aren't growing, you are dying. You have the power to decide who you are. You can choose to be stuck in the same mindset, never growing, never learning, never evolving. You can also choose to grow, seeking new opportunities and perspectives, challenging yourself, becoming more confident, and building new relationships.

The Role of Confidence

Confidence is a powerful byproduct of realizing your power. When you recognize that you have the ability to influence your life, make decisions, and take control of your actions, your confidence naturally grows. Confidence isn't about arrogance; it's about trusting in your ability to handle whatever comes your way. Eventually, confidence leads to self-validation. Before long, you are in total control and taking complete power over yourself.

This process starts by using your power in small, everyday situations. Small, intentional choices like taking a walk or eating better soon become bigger choices, like going to the gym or giving in less frequently to cravings for junk food. Over time, those small choices lead to bigger ones, and your confidence begins to grow.

With confidence, you can overcome obstacles and not have major setbacks. With confidence, one missed gym day doesn't become two. One cheat meal doesn't become three. Overcoming obstacles and challenging limiting beliefs leads to making empowered choices. You will begin to trust yourself more. Over time, this trust will build into lasting confidence and power.

Taking the Step into Power

Changing your view on power and getting a new perspective doesn't happen overnight; it's a journey. Gaining self-awareness, self-confidence, and realization of the power you hold takes practice, intention, patience, self-reflection, and the willingness to take the first step. It means acknowledging that you have the power to create the life you want and that you are worthy of success, love, and fulfillment.

Do you know what it takes? It takes the power of perception. Self-awareness is just the first step. Just like any other journey, using the power of your perception takes practice, which means many more steps like self-reflection, self-confidence, a growth mindset, and intentionality.

The same is true when building a house. As a carpenter or builder, you start with a blueprint. This blueprint guides you, just as our choices guide our personal journeys. We have a blueprint that outlines where we will place the walls, how far apart the studs will be, and the amount of flooring we need. But what happens next? Inevitably, there is a change to discuss: the tile is no longer available, the wall leaves a too-narrow hallway, or a space becomes the perfect place to add shelves or a closet not previously planned.

When my youngest daughter was born, we needed more space. With the help of a friend of mine, I decided to build an addition on my house. We had a blueprint, but things changed throughout the project. There was a plan for the foundation, but we realized a few extra feet would make the entire process a bit easier.

Once the walls went up, we made adjustments to the locations of electrical outlets, windows, and doors. We added closet space after finding extra room when measuring the bathroom fixtures. As we worked, things changed and evolved. We adapted as decisions needed to change or simply didn't seem to work as well in reality as they did in planning.

Kids do this when building houses out of blocks. If you've ever had a child who loves building with blocks, or been one, you know the joy of sitting down with a collection of pieces and creating something uniquely your own. The process requires flexibility and the ability to adapt on the fly.

They begin by laying bricks, and before they know it, they have constructed a wall. Then they notice a window that looks appealing and decide to incorporate it. As they continue building, they pause to think: *This is the perfect spot for the door*. After adding one, they then resume building the walls until they've completed the entire house.

Interestingly, they didn't even start with much of a blueprint; instead, they began with a simple idea and adapted as they found the various pieces along the way. This flexibility enabled them to successfully construct their building. This ability to harness creativity and find balance is what it's all about.

This adaptability is crucial. When working with a contractor, things need to adapt as the blueprint is put into practice. When you walk into any LEGO store, you'll often find a large table filled with random LEGO pieces. Children can sit there and start creating without a predefined blueprint; they begin with just an idea and dive into building their own house.

In either situation, things start with a plan, but it must be adapted based on available resources or feedback from the people involved in the project. The same is true in life. We must realize that while we definitely have a plan to start with, we must be flexible and adapt as external forces, internal beliefs, and various other aspects of life change.

As you step into your power, you will notice shifts in how you carry yourself, interact with others, and approach challenges. You will no longer feel like a passive observer of your life; you will feel like an active participant, shaping your own destiny.

In the next chapter, we'll explore the responsible use of power. Specifically, we'll look at how to use it wisely and ethically, ensuring it aligns with your values and contributes positively to the world around you.

Reflection Questions

1. When do you feel most powerful in your daily life? What thoughts, choices, or behaviors contribute to that feeling?
2. Think about a recent situation where you felt powerless. Looking back, what choices were still available to you in that moment?
3. What is one small decision you can make this week that reflects confidence in your ability to shape your actions and direction in life?

CHAPTER 10

RESPONSIBLE USE OF POWER

Power, when used responsibly, can be one of the most transformative forces in our lives and in society.

However, power comes with significant responsibility. If you're a fan of Spider-Man, you might remember that Uncle Ben once said, "With great power comes great responsibility." This is the foundation of our discussion. We have a responsibility to ensure that our use of power is ethical.

This requires the right mindset. The way we use our power can have far-reaching consequences—not only for ourselves but also for others. It's not enough to simply recognize our power; we must also understand how to use it to promote good, encourage growth, and respect others' dignity and autonomy.

Earlier, we discussed how our reactions can differ based on who is giving us feedback, whether it's a friend, family member, or boss. That difference highlights the importance of accountability. At any moment, we have the choice regarding how to respond to feedback. We can choose to hold our contempt and emotions, or we can let it all out. We can choose to keep our composure and take a moment to reflect, or we can react and face the consequences. These moments are where we exercise our true power.

In this chapter, we will explore what it means to use power responsibly, how to align our power with our values, and how to ensure that our actions reflect integrity, empathy, and respect. Building on the previous concepts, we will dive into how to ensure we are acting responsibly in the use of power and that our actions reflect the perception we are trying to portray. We will move from simply understanding the things in our lives that shape the lens through which we view the world to understanding how our actions shape how the world perceives us.

The Ethical Foundation of Power

At its core, responsible power is built on ethics, on doing what is right, just, and fair. Ethics is the guiding principle that determines how power is exercised. When we use power ethically, we make decisions that consider the well-being of others, the long-term impact of our actions, and the greater good.

When power is used irresponsibly, we promote ourselves at the cost of diminishing, demeaning, and alienating others. When used responsibly, we foster long-term, sustainable development in ourselves and those around us. When used irresponsibly, any growth achieved is only short-lived and at the expense of those around us.

Ethical power is not about manipulating others to achieve our personal goals or using force to control situations. It's about exercising influence in a way that is respectful, transparent, and aligned with our core values. As mentioned earlier, true power lies within ourselves. That internal control, combined with intentionality, gives us even greater external power to influence the world and people around us.

When we approach power with an ethical mindset, we ensure our actions align with the principles of honesty, fairness, and accountability. We ask ourselves: *Is this decision in the best interest of everyone involved? Am I using my power to elevate others or to suppress them?* Our actions reflect our beliefs and views of the world around us. They should portray our intended message.

A great example of this is often seen in children's sports, but it applies to all sports. I'm specifically referring to what I call "bleacher coaches." We all know who they are: those parents sitting in the stands who believe their child is the next Babe Ruth, Wayne Gretzky, Caitlin Clark, LeBron James, Kobe Bryant, or Michael Jordan.

They yell and criticize everything the referees do and question the decisions of the coaches, like why their child wasn't played or why they were taken out of the game at a specific time. You can hear them voicing their opinions about referees, insisting that a call was unjust and should have gone the other way. This behavior is common in today's society and often extends to professional sports as well.

As fans, we pay hundreds of dollars to watch our teams play. When they don't win, we might find ourselves yelling at the referees from the stands. But why do we engage in this criticism? What is the expected result? A call to be reversed or points to be added to the score?

The reality is that, in professional sports, the players and referees often can't hear our individual voices. They only hear the collective noise of the crowd. So, when we shout, "You should have skated better!" or "That was a bad call!" it doesn't truly reach them.

As a coach, I emphasize to both my players and their parents that it is our responsibility as a team not to leave the outcome of the game in anyone else's hands, especially not the referees'. You will not hear me yelling at referees during a game. While watching a game, I may engage in conversations with those around me, but you won't necessarily notice. The reason is that I can't recall a single instance where a parent in the stands yelled at a referee, and the referee responded by saying, "You know what? You're absolutely right. That was a bad call. I think I'm going to change my mind." It simply doesn't happen.

This behavior stems from a lack of awareness about the power we possess. At those moments, we are not focused on building relationships; instead, we are fixated on one individual, one issue, and our own wants, desires, needs, hopes, and dreams. We fail to pause and reflect on how we can inspire through our influence.

True power lies in our ability to build relationships. Rather than setting a good example, building relationships, and having a positive influence, actions like yelling from the stands lead to discrediting, distrust, and alienating others. I have heard very few fans or parents say, "I would really like to have a deeper conversation with that person yelling at the players, coaches, and referees."

Instead of fostering connections, actions like these actually damage them. The more we yell from the stands, the more others around us think: *What an idiot! I will never ask that person for advice about anything.* This prevents us from forging new relationships and can even undermine existing ones.

It's common for acquaintances to evolve into more meaningful connections in which we genuinely impact someone's life. You can see this on the other side of the lens. It is likely someone is speaking up and telling the person next to them, "I can't believe they are yelling like that. It is so frustrating." The other person responds, and before long, a relationship forms. Both agree that the behavior is wrong and start to find out what else they agree on. This relationship builds trust and understanding, while the person yelling has alienated themselves from others.

When we behave in this manner in our daily lives and fail to practice accountability, we neglect the long-term potential of our influence. We miss the opportunity for self-reflection, which is crucial for developing self-awareness. By understanding our actions, we can begin to build relationships, use our power responsibly, and inspire those around us.

The point is, what is the result of criticizing a referee from the stands? Where is the greater good? No matter what call was made and how it affected your favorite team, you have the power to interpret that situation and react. You can either keep your power by realizing it is just a game and reframing your interpretation, or you can give your power away by acting foolishly and losing the ability to positively influence those around you.

The Importance of Integrity

Using power responsibly requires integrity. Our internal value system decides what lines we are willing to cross when making decisions. Integrity tells us what we consider acceptable behavior and what isn't, which in turn guides the actions we choose.

Pretend you are walking down the street by yourself and see a $100 bill lying on the ground. You look up, and nobody is around for blocks. Do you put the money in your pocket or look a bit harder for the owner? Maybe you even turn it in to the closest authority in case someone comes back asking for it. The answer you choose is based on your integrity. Some find it perfectly acceptable to claim any lost item, while others think efforts should be made to locate the owner.

Integrity is what ensures that your actions align with your personal beliefs and values. If you believe in the mantra "finders keepers," there is no hesitation in putting the money in your pocket. On the other hand, if you empathize with "losers, weepers," you might look harder to find the owner. Whether you decide to keep the money or turn it in, you aren't wrong; you are simply acting in alignment with your integrity.

This is why understanding your own perception is so important. Without first understanding your own thoughts, feelings, and preferences, you can't interact honestly and authentically with others. Without acknowledging and accepting what makes you unique, you can't open up, build trust, and form connections. Integrity builds credibility, and credibility is the foundation of true power. Without integrity, power is hollow and fleeting.

A lack of integrity, on the other hand, can lead to abuse of power. Power wielded without integrity often involves dishonesty, exploitation, or manipulation, eroding trust and leading to disempowerment.

This is the epitome of the power cycle. Believing that power exists externally takes away integrity and, in turn, honesty and authenticity. Without these, you rely on external validation through power, money, and status, leaving you with superficial relationships, very little influence, and a tendency to act in ways that gain more external power. Power comes only through authentic relationships, not through exploitation and manipulation.

Using Your Power to Empower Others

Using power responsibly involves empowering others. We discussed earlier how power is not something to take away from others but something that is renewable and achievable through connection and relationships.

We also discussed the importance of self-awareness. This is more than just knowing your own beliefs. Being able to recognize your own strengths and weaknesses allows you to partner with others to both offer and receive help. Collaboration creates stronger bonds, which in turn lead to even more power. Strong relationships provide the power to influence, to build people up, and to grow.

By using your power to form connections and build relationships, you create a positive cycle of empowerment. You empower others to reach their goals, and they do the same for you. This cycle creates a ripple effect that is often not fully understood.

So many times in life, an opportunity arises simply through how we interact with others. Even writing this book is a great example. I had an idea, but this is the realization of the power of relationships. In nursing school, I went to Bolivia on a mission trip that provided medical care to remote villages.

Through this, I made a connection with someone who became a friend. Years later, I got the idea to write this book and reached out to him because I knew he had experience in this area. His response was to connect me with another friend of his who had more recent experience. Through this interaction, I found my way to get this idea to you.

Empowering others doesn't mean giving up your own power; it means sharing it, creating a collaborative dynamic where everyone's strengths are recognized and valued.

Throughout this book, we've discussed how power is often viewed as having control over someone or something. We need to change that perspective to one that emphasizes having power *with* others.

True power comes from relationships. It's in these connections that real growth and change occur. Engaging in kind, loving, and understanding conversations with someone who holds a different viewpoint is vital. Meeting on common ground doesn't mean you have to change your perspective, but it does involve mutual respect. That is where genuine power exists: in collaborating with others.

As you build these relationships, you'll find that your influence grows. Power with others stems from these connections. When you demonstrate your ability to foster relationships, people will begin to rely on you and be more open to listening to your perspectives in the future. True power is about empowering others. It's about providing people with the space to express themselves and respecting their right to be heard. Ultimately, it comes down to accountability for your actions. Admitting your mistakes doesn't mean you are incompetent; it means you are human.

Accountability is empowering. When you recognize that your actions didn't align with your integrity, you not only grow but also allow others to feel heard. Creating a space where people feel heard and respected fosters understanding and a sense of value. When people feel valued, they feel empowered. They feel safe to express their thoughts, emotions, and ideas.

When this happens, power is amplified by the many ways people can work together. For example, a leader who uses their power to inspire and mentor their team members doesn't diminish their influence. Instead, they amplify it. When others feel valued and empowered, they become more engaged, motivated, and willing to contribute to collective success.

The Role of Accountability

Accountability is a key aspect of responsible power. When we have power, we must be willing to answer for our actions and their impact. This means being open to feedback, admitting when we've made mistakes, and taking responsibility for the consequences of our choices.

We don't always like the consequences of our actions. Good or bad, we must be accountable for our actions. This can be easy when they lead to positive outcomes: a promotion, helping someone out, or achieving our goals. It is also important to have accountability when our actions don't have the intended impact. When we harm relationships with words, leave someone out of the group, or make a mistake, we must be accountable.

Accountability provides reparation and prevents one mistake from becoming a cycle.

Earlier, we talked about the fact that there is always a choice. Each choice has a consequence. You may not always like the consequences, but you always have a choice. Accountability is accepting consequences, which allows you to learn and grow. If the consequence is the criticism you received, accountability allows you to use the information as a growth opportunity. If your actions led to something great, accountability helps others want to do the same.

Furthermore, accountability helps keep our power in check. It ensures we don't misuse or abuse our influence and helps us stay grounded in the reality of our actions. Without accountability, it's easy to fall into the trap of entitlement or arrogance, believing that our power is limitless or that we are above reproach. As much as we need self-accountability, we also need others' accountability. Alcoholics Anonymous is very successful at helping people obtain and sustain sobriety. That is because each new member is assigned a sponsor for accountability.

Being accountable also means holding others to the same standard. You must be willing to call out unethical behavior and ensure that those around you are also acting responsibly. This creates a culture of mutual respect and integrity. Confronting others is not easy, especially in our current culture, where "ghosting" is the norm rather than having a conversation and offering feedback. It takes relationship building and enough self-accountability to handle it when others give you the same feedback.

Avoiding Power over Others

One of the most important aspects of responsible power is recognizing the danger of exercising power *over* others. Power *over* others is about domination, control, and manipulation. Power *with* others is about collaboration and mutual respect. Power over others comes from a perspective of fear; a fear of being powerless leads to seeking external sources of power. Power with others comes from confidence: being self-aware and self-confident enough to engage the world around you and grow. Power over others manifests as control and dominion, while power with others manifests as empathy and compassion.

This is often seen in business. Leaders who use power *over* others often have higher turnover and employee burnout. This scenario would look like a leader who uses coercion, threats, or intimidation to get results. Employees who don't comply will be punished. The focus is more on productivity and results rather than employee satisfaction.

A leader who uses power *with* others will engage employees and seek their input. Time and again, this method is shown to be more impactful than the first. By engaging employees and hearing their voices, this leader can get to the heart of any productivity issues by hearing from those who do the job. In this scenario, productivity increases while burnout and turnover decrease. Employees are more efficient because they want to do their jobs well and find ways to be more productive. The company also saves money because happy employees tend to stay longer, decreasing the costs of training new employees.

The Power of Self-Reflection

Since true power is internal, responsible use involves regular self-reflection. Checking in to see whether your actions align with your values and beliefs is important to do regularly. You should consistently ask yourself: *How am I using my power? Is it aligned with my values? Am I being fair and just in my actions?*

Self-reflection helps you stay grounded and ensures you're not acting out of ego, insecurity, or unchecked ambition.

When you regularly reflect on your use of power, you create space for growth. You can identify areas where you might be misusing your influence or need to correct course. Self-awareness keeps you humble, mindful, and focused on using your power for good.

The Long-Term Impact of Power

Finally, responsible power takes into account the long-term impact of our actions. It's easy to get caught up in short-term gains, immediate rewards, or quick fixes. However, true power is about creating sustainable, positive change that lasts.

We spent much of this chapter discussing just that. While some people seem able to exert power by exploiting and manipulating others, it never lasts. They are either caught and lose their ability to manipulate or are forced to bounce from relationship to relationship to keep up the success of their antics.

Consider the difference between a coach and a mentor. In conversations about sports, we often joke about "bleacher coaches," those who shout advice from the sidelines. But what does a real coach do?

I have experience in both coaching and mentoring. Currently, I'm coaching a recreational league team that includes one of my children. I will be interacting with these young adults for a few weeks, aiming to help them grow and improve. As I practice with the team, my goal is to help them improve their physical performance. It's ultimately a short-term objective, focused on a brief interaction. Over the next few weeks, my aim is to prepare them to win the league by the end of the year.

In contrast, when I mentor someone in a professional environment, that's a long-term relationship. That's the key difference. Coaches typically focus on short-term outcomes, such as winning the next game, improving over the season, or winning the championship at the end. Mentors, on the other hand, look at the long-term picture.

While my role as a coach is based on short-term interaction and goals, my role as a nurse leader in healthcare focuses on the long-term growth of people and programs. I help people take steps toward advancing their careers. This process is not just a few weeks long; it involves ongoing support. Regular check-ins and updates are essential to ensuring the plan adapts to new information.

Mentoring typically takes years. During this stretch, goals and opportunities can change. If the plan doesn't reflect these changes, goals cannot be achieved. Even with programs, there is planning, implementation, evaluation, and adaptation. Projects I participate in often take months to get going and much longer to become sustainable.

The distinction between coaches and mentors is significant. Although some coaches do become mentors and develop long-lasting relationships with us, it is the mentor who fosters deeper connections and influences others over time. When someone achieves great things, they don't often recall that one coach they had for just a few weeks. Instead, they remember the mentor who has been a guiding presence throughout a substantial part of their life and helped set them on their path.

When we use power responsibly, we think beyond the present moment and consider the lasting effects of our choices. We ask: *What will the consequences of this decision be in the future? How will this decision affect others in the long run?* When used responsibly, power leads to both personal good and greater good. Responsible use of power leads to self-growth and the ability to positively influence the world around you. Considering others is necessary for building relationships and connections that enable influence.

Just as the pursuit of power is a journey, its use should be for long-term, not short-term, impact. Power should not be used just to stay calm now but for what will happen later when you keep your composure time and again. Rarely does someone ever reach their goals after one single act. Often, it is a journey with several steps along the way. Keeping long-term goals in mind not only helps with short-term actions but also with achieving success.

My wife has worked with children of various needs throughout her life. Each step has led to her current success. This is only due to the consistency of her actions, as she is self-aware and self-confident. She didn't just work with these kids one time; she worked with them in many capacities over more than two decades. Because every reaction was built on empathy, compassion, and understanding, she has been able to create a program in our church where children with all kinds of needs can attend at their own abilities. I have seen parents walk up to her in tears to express their gratitude. This would not have been successful without consistent actions over time.

Understanding this new definition of "true" power is essential. In the next chapter, we will explore the hidden dynamics behind the power chase and pull back the curtain on its superficial appeal, revealing new possibilities.

Reflection Questions

1. Think about a recent situation where you had influence over others. How did you choose to use that influence, and what impact did it have on the people around you?
2. In your relationships, do you tend to exercise power over others or power with others through collaboration and respect? What might change if you focused more on empowering those around you?
3. What is one way you can intentionally use your influence this week to support, encourage, or empower someone else?

CHAPTER 11

THE ILLUSION OF POWER

Power is often seen as visible, but it is more often invisible.

Power is a lot like a magic trick. We are in awe of the outward appearance of the woman being cut in half or the man levitating. The reality is, the power is in the sleight of hand. The box is built so that the woman folds into one half, while a pair of fake legs extends from the other half. The man is likely using magnets or wires we can't see. Either way, we are more focused on the entertainment of the illusion than the limitations of reality.

With power, it is important to focus on the reality behind the scenes rather than on the attraction of the illusion. We need to focus less on the illusion that we can control things around us and more on the fact that we can only control ourselves.

We've discussed how pursuing power can actually lead us to lose control. We have the choice to drive that car or not, and that is where our power truly exists. In reality, we have no control over when the lights change, how other drivers drive, or the weather, which can make driving more or less safe. An accident or a flat tire could happen, and we have little power over these situations.

We do, however, have power in how we respond. This highlights the illusion we are trying to challenge. Our real power comes from our choices and actions. We have the ability to distinguish between perception and reality. We can choose to ask ourselves: *Is my reality the same as objective reality?* Recognizing and challenging this illusion is where true power resides. This recognition allows us to pause and reflect. It enables us to dig deeper into why we make certain decisions or feel a particular way.

While some wield their power overtly, others do so subtly, and some even create the illusion of power without possessing any real control. This illusion can be intoxicating, blinding us to the truth about ourselves and others. The danger lies in mistaking the appearance of power for its true essence, leading to decisions based on false assumptions and ultimately reinforcing a cycle of insecurity and mistrust.

We are too often drawn to what we perceive as power. We gravitate toward those who seem able to command things into reality or make things happen. It bears repeating that true power is internal and everyone has it. Only through control and responsible use of internal power can you achieve true external power.

In this chapter, we'll examine the illusion of power, its psychological effects, and how we can navigate this illusion to access and wield true power in our lives.

The False Symbols of Power

In many societies, people are conditioned to associate power with external symbols such as wealth, status, position, titles, and material possessions. We think of power as being able to make things happen simply by saying so. These symbols can make someone appear powerful, but they don't always reflect the actual depth of their influence or control.

Remember, even if someone exerts any of these outside forces on you, power lies in controlling your reaction to them, not in being able to dictate them. Think of any political landscape. Each politician attempts to exert their power of money by running ads to slander the opponent. In reality, the power lies in the response of the opponent and voters: either play along or ignore it completely.

For example, a CEO of a large corporation may have immense wealth and a prestigious title, but does that necessarily mean they have true power? True power goes beyond external trappings. It's about the ability to influence, inspire, and create change, qualities that may not always be visible through superficial markers.

We perceive them as powerful because they control the company and make a lot of money from it. They set policies and decide how the company will operate. Their true power, however, lies in influencing those around them. If employees don't want to stay because of how they are treated, there will be no company to run.

Sure, many employees will simply stay because they need the money. Without an engaging environment, they will leave as soon as someone else offers them the money they need. Worse, employees in this type of environment often work less efficiently, as they are less motivated to do someone else's work because "they are the CEO, and they said so."

The illusion of power often arises when we mistake these external symbols for the true essence of power. Someone may project an image of confidence and control, but beneath the surface, they may be insecure or lack genuine influence. Worse, they may be overconfident with no meaningful relationships.

Understanding the difference between external appearances and true power is crucial for maintaining clarity and making informed decisions about how we use our own power. To set the tone for the rest of this chapter, I will repeat: true power is only an internal force, and everyone has it!

The Role of Fear in the Illusion of Power

One of the key factors that contributes to the illusion of power is fear. When people are afraid, whether of losing control, being judged, or facing uncertainty, they may resort to tactics that create an appearance of power.

We don't talk back at work for fear of losing our jobs. We may not bring up concerns in a relationship for fear of making someone mad or damaging the relationship. We don't take care of ourselves out of fear of what others may think.

People attempting to exert external power may engage in behaviors like bullying, intimidation, or manipulation to maintain a façade of dominance, even if they're deeply insecure. Remember, it is just a façade. Most of this comes from their fear of being seen as weak or powerless. Only they can control their actions based on their feelings, not you.

Why do so many bullies stop when someone stands up to them? They really just want to be perceived as strong and powerful so they can cover up their own fears and insecurities. We often do this in life. How many times have you joined in when others laughed at you just so they didn't know you were really hurting?

Not only does having a fear-driven approach take power away, but it is also unsustainable. It relies on external control mechanisms, such as forcing people to comply out of fear or using deceit to maintain influence.

As mentioned in other chapters, such influence does not last. This false power is incredibly fleeting. Fear-driven power creates a toxic environment that can lead to resistance, mistrust, and eventual rebellion. It destroys the relationships needed to achieve true power, internal and external. It destroys self-realization and accountability, and it undermines relationships with others.

In contrast, true power doesn't come from instilling fear. It comes from self-assurance, empathy, and the ability to lead with integrity. When power is rooted in authenticity and respect, it is not dependent on maintaining a façade. True power can weather challenges without resorting to fear-based tactics.

Think of any story about a large corporation and how it started. Computer companies started out of garages. When the founders wanted to take their idea to the world, their influence didn't come from external power; it came from relationships. Relationships led them to the people who would finally take a chance and invest money. Banks don't tend to give out money until you already have it. When the time came to market and sell the computers, it was relationships that convinced others to sell something nobody thought they needed.

The Power of Perception vs. Reality

The perception of power can be just as influential as actual power. We often base our decisions, relationships, and interactions on how we perceive others' power (or worse, anticipated reactions). For example, a person who appears confident and authoritative may be assumed to have more power than someone who is quieter or more reserved, even though their actual influence may be less significant.

Have you ever walked up to someone in a store and asked for help, only to realize they didn't work there? Why? Because of how they dressed and acted. They gave the impression of someone who knew the store and its products and may even have looked the part.

The danger of lacking self-awareness about how we form our perceptions is that we end up making assumptions about people and situations that aren't always accurate. We begin to simply see the homeless person as someone who made poor choices rather than someone we can help. We see our boss as someone who can control whether we receive a raise or promotion, not someone who can collaborate on our work. We see someone in expensive clothes and an exotic car as someone with influence, rather than as someone who may need a meaningful connection more than anyone. Without understanding the true source of power, it is easy to be persuaded by external forces.

Similarly, we may believe that we lack power simply because we don't fit the typical mold of a powerful individual. But power is not determined solely by appearances. True power lies in the ability to influence, adapt, and make meaningful decisions, regardless of how others perceive us.

Power is the ability to stay true to ourselves and be confident in our actions. It is the ability to control how we interpret information and situations and how we respond. Power is about doing great work, no matter the title we hold. It is about treating everyone with empathy, compassion, and respect, whether they can immediately help us or not.

The Illusion of Control

One of the most common illusions of power is the belief that we can control everything around us. It was mentioned earlier how power is often seen as the ability to control. This illusion is especially pervasive among people in positions of leadership or authority.

The idea that control equals power can be seductive, but it is ultimately flawed. No one can control every variable, person, or outcome. Life is unpredictable, and attempting to exert absolute control can lead to frustration, burnout, and a sense of helplessness when things inevitably don't go according to plan.

We have seen this recently with large-scale technology outages. We think we are in control as we go about our day, only for a simple service outage to suddenly prevent us from working, shopping, watching television, or performing a number of other tasks planned for the day. We thought we had control over our jobs until our computer stopped working. We thought we had control over our viewing habits until streaming was no longer an option.

True power, then, is not about control. It's about adaptability, resilience, and the ability to respond effectively to changing circumstances. Leaders who recognize that they can't control everything are often the most powerful because they know how to inspire others, make thoughtful decisions in the face of uncertainty, and adapt when things don't go as expected.

Power is about how you responded when the global service outage occurred. Power is choosing to try every device to see what still works or to pick up a book.

The Illusion of Power in Social Media and Public Personas

In the age of social media, the illusion of power has taken on new dimensions. Platforms like Instagram, Twitter, and LinkedIn allow people to curate highly controlled images of their lives and their success. With the right photos, the right messaging, and the right network, anyone can project an image of power and influence. We've even created new jobs around this, as people are now officially being labeled "influencers" just for using these social media platforms.

But the power we see online is often just that: an image. Behind the polished posts and curated feeds, people may struggle with the same doubts, insecurities, and challenges as anyone else. The illusion of power created by social media can be dangerous, as it encourages us to compare ourselves to others and aspire to a power that is unattainable or superficial.

How many times have you seen this happen to famous people? So many beloved and popular people have fallen from grace because a hidden, dirty secret was brought to light or they expressed a personal view that didn't fit the societal norm. Look at all the Hollywood people who were shown to manipulate women in the industry, the politicians who have been put in jail when their bad practices are revealed, or people in positions of "power" stripped of their titles due to hidden addictions or their support (or opposition) of political events. An image is great, but the truth will eventually shine.

It's important to recognize that what we see online is not always the full picture. People may seem powerful because of their online presence, but this power may not translate into real-world influence or satisfaction. Understanding this distinction can help us avoid being misled by the illusion of power in the digital world.

Today, people even inflate their presence and perceived influence through fake accounts or artificial intelligence programs that generate likes, comments, and followers. Some of the most viral videos show how people create those perfect social media posts through illusions and deception. Camera angles, picture editing, and props are used to create that perfect image and hide the real situation.

Danger of the Power Trap

Perhaps the greatest danger in the illusion of defining power as external is the trap it creates. When we buy into the idea that we have to gain power through external sources, we fall into the trap of the power chase. Basing power on the illusion of the external, such as symbols, fear tactics, and social media personas, disconnects us from the truth. Being disconnected from the truth not only distracts from the internal power we already possess, but it also leaves us feeling frustrated, unhappy, and unfulfilled.

Aside from negative feelings, we have negative actions. When we focus on the external and conform to what the world defines as power, our actions don't align with our views. Constantly conforming to others prevents the self-awareness needed to gain a confident perspective on our individual values and beliefs. Without realizing and accepting who we are, we lack the ability to be authentic. Without authenticity, relationships become superficial, and connection is almost impossible. When we cling to what the world views as power, we prevent the actualization of our internal power.

Internal power is grounded in authenticity, humility, and the ability to adapt. Uncertainties in life are inevitable. Building relationships through authentic connections and remaining humble to gain insight allows us to adapt when life changes our path.

Power isn't gained and hoarded; it is renewable and shared. It's the ability to decide to react positively or negatively. It's controlling your reactions to influence the people and world around you. It is creating positive change in the environment rather than letting the environment change and control you.

Recognizing the Illusion of Power

We see this illusion prominently in magic. Despite our fascination with it, we generally understand that magic is not real; it's simply an illusion. We even refer to it as "the art of illusion." This captivates us in movies, where we become deeply engaged because we want the experience to feel real. Films like the *Harry Potter* movies and fantasy realms like those in the *Lord of the Rings* series showcase magic, allowing us to escape into those illusions for a while.

We can see this phenomenon in real life. We willingly pay to attend magic shows and watch performers execute fascinating tricks. For instance, they might saw a lady in half, perform stunts with a tiger, or make someone disappear. Sometimes, they even pull someone from the audience to participate. They'll place this person in a cage, cover it, spin it around, and then, *poof,* the person vanishes. We find this absolutely thrilling and are thoroughly entertained by the illusion.

However, this also happens in real life when we are captivated by the notion that power resides with one person rather than another. Often, we get so caught up in this illusion that we forget to pause and reflect.

The key difference here is that after a magic show, we typically acknowledge the tricks for what they are. We might say, "That was an amazing trick, but I know it's not real." We consciously recognize the mechanics behind it.

There was a show featuring the famous magicians Penn and Teller, focused on whether they could be fooled. In this show, various magicians would demonstrate their tricks, and Penn and Teller, being experts in sleight of hand and other techniques, would explain how each trick worked, unless they were genuinely puzzled.

This experience highlights a crucial point: we have the ability to pause and acknowledge that a trick is just that: a trick. While it may be entertaining, it lacks real substance. The real power in a magic show lies in the illusion itself, much like a rabbit appearing to materialize from a hat due to clever prearrangements hidden inside. We can do the same in our everyday lives. It's essential to pause and recognize that much of what we perceive as power may be an illusion. Understanding our perceptions and learning to control them is true power because it gives us the ability to control our choices.

Internal awareness is about avoiding the trap of the illusion of external power. Being aware of how power is often distorted and manipulated helps us to see our relationship with it. Awareness helps us determine if we are conforming to external power or exercising the force of our internal power.

Here are a few questions to ask yourself when considering the power dynamics in your life:

- *Am I chasing external symbols of power (wealth, status, etc.) because I believe they will give me happiness or fulfillment?*
- *Do I use fear or control tactics to maintain a sense of power?*
- *Am I comparing myself to others' public personas, assuming they have power because of what they project?*
- *How does the power I hold truly affect others? Is it creating positive change or fostering insecurity?*

Being able to answer these questions honestly will help you determine whether you are acting on the assumption that power is external or are aware that it lies within you. Once you accept that power is internal, these self-reflection questions can help you untangle the illusion of power and capture its true essence.

Being humble and grounded in the understanding that you control only your actions will help unlock the secret behind the magic tricks. Just like with magic, everyone will be caught in awe of your different perspective, giving you the power of influence.

The next chapter will elaborate on the idea of control and searching for it internally. It will focus on recognizing our limits and setting boundaries. Taking control over our perceptions is truly powerful.

Reflection Questions

1. What external symbols of power do you find yourself most influenced by, such as titles, wealth, status, appearance, or social media presence? Why do those symbols affect you?
2. Think about a time when you assumed someone had more power than they actually did. How did that perception shape your thoughts, choices, or behavior? What could you have done to focus instead on your response, adaptability, and choices?
3. In what areas of your life might you be mistaking the appearance of control for real power?

CHAPTER 12

CONTROL WHAT YOU CAN CONTROL

We cannot control the environment around us; we can only control our personal response to it.

We've talked a lot about illusions, particularly the illusions of control and power. Power often creates this illusion of control. Now let's focus on what you can actually control.

It all starts with recognizing those illusions, identifying what's real, and concentrating on that. You cannot control other people. You can't dictate how someone thinks of you or how they drive around you. You also can't control what they read, the websites they visit, or what they post on social media.

However, what you can control is yourself. You can control your mindset, actions, habits, emotions, and responses. You can set boundaries and decide how to respond to a social media post. While you cannot control the content of that post, you can control your reaction to it. You have power over what you choose to view, what you watch, and where you get your information.

One of the greatest lessons in life is learning to accept what is outside of our control while focusing our energy on what we can influence. When we attempt to control every aspect of our lives, we become overwhelmed, frustrated, and disempowered.

True empowerment comes from knowing where our influence ends and where it begins and then investing our time and energy in those areas where we can make a meaningful impact.

In this chapter, we'll explore the concept of control, the importance of recognizing its limits, and practical ways to focus on what we can actually change.

The Illusion of Total Control

Many of us harbor the belief that we must control every aspect of our lives to be successful or happy. We believe that if we can just manage every detail, predict every outcome, and prevent every obstacle, we will have a sense of security and stability. We plan our day by filling our schedules, planning our commute, setting our alarms, and deciding what food to eat.

External control is an illusion. Life is full of uncertainty and unplanned events. There will always be external factors that infringe on our lives. Control is not over these external things, but over how we interpret and react to them.

When we cling to the belief that we have control over anything other than our own perceptions, we are setting ourselves up for disappointment. We have no control over the weather, the economy, or other people's actions. We can't even always control how they interpret our well-thought-out words. That meeting may get canceled, a traffic crash can alter our commute, an overnight power outage can stop that alarm from sounding on time, and that food may not sit well in your stomach today. You may even hurt someone with your words, despite your best intentions.

Accepting this realization is often difficult because it is scary. After all, if we have no control, why make plans? However, accepting the reality that you only control the internal should actually be liberating! Knowing that your only control is internal frees you from relying on the external for happiness.

Make your plans, but humbly acknowledge they may change. Take comfort in your ability to control how you interpret and respond to change, as it allows you to focus on what really matters most. Embracing the uncertainty brings so many wonderful things you may not have experienced otherwise. Enjoy the detour, as it allows you to see things you may not have seen before or listen to that podcast a little longer.

Would you have danced in the rain if you'd brought your umbrella? Would you have enjoyed that song playing as you pulled into the parking lot if you weren't stuck in traffic? I know I likely wouldn't even be writing this book if I hadn't taken a trip to another country. Control your choices and let the rest go.

Focusing on Inner Change

While there are many things beyond our control, there is still plenty we can influence. Our thoughts, actions, and responses are all areas where we have the greatest power. By directing our energy toward these internal elements, we can create positive change in our lives and in the lives of others.

Internal change is all about you:

- **Your mindset**: You can choose how you perceive and react to situations. A fixed mindset stays rigid and stuck in the past. It closes the door on new perspectives and opportunities. A growth mindset opens up new possibilities and fosters resilience. You get to choose which one you will use: the autopilot of the fixed mindset or the liberation of the growth mindset.
- **Your actions**: No matter the circumstance, you can choose your response. You have the power to be intentional with your actions or rely on reactions to get you through life. The difference is in your choice of mindset. A fixed mindset operates on bias, assumptions, and

emotions, guided by reactions and stunting growth, while an open mindset allows you to pause, reflect, and act intentionally. You choose whether your actions reflect your goals and values or those of someone else.

- **Your habits**: Daily routines you choose determine the cycle you are in. You can either develop healthy habits, like exercising, practicing mindfulness, or setting time aside to build relationships, or unhealthy ones, like eating junk food, spending too much time on screens, or keeping yourself away from others. Your choice will determine whether you fall into the destructive cycle of the power chase or the constructive cycle of seeking new perspectives.
- **Your emotional responses:** Similar to actions, you choose how much you let things affect you emotionally. Your choice, however, doesn't rely on feeling a certain way but on how you express that feeling. For example, if someone betrays your trust, you are going to get upset. You should feel this way. The control lies in how you respond when you're upset. You can choose to accept the mistrust and work to rebuild, never talk to that person again, or even act out in revenge.
- **Your boundaries**: Setting boundaries will determine how well you manage your emotions once you recognize them. You need to set limits with yourself and with others. Determining when to confront a situation and when to simply avoid it is important when emotions feel overwhelming.

Focusing on these areas will help build consistent internal health even when things are difficult. Choosing the right mindset sets the stage to choose your actions. Daily habits will help determine how much control you have when emotions change your perspective. Setting boundaries will help maintain healthy habits.

You can control your expressions. You can change your habits. You can take a deep breath and remain calm. You are the only one who can set boundaries with the world and the people around you.

The Power of Acceptance

One of the most empowering practices is learning to accept the things you cannot control. This doesn't mean giving up or resigning yourself to passivity; rather, it means recognizing the limits of your power and choosing to let go of what you cannot change.

This comes through changing your mindset. If you are preoccupied with every tiny detail, you will worry yourself into an eventual downfall. Instead of hyper-focusing on small things, step back and consider other possibilities. In essence, you don't control the world around you, and true power lies in accepting that reality.

A common analogy is the stages of grief. People often start with feelings of anger and frustration, but acceptance is the final stage. Why is acceptance so important? Because it signifies that you've come to terms with the fact that you cannot control certain aspects of life, such as a medical diagnosis. You can't control the outcome, and ultimately, we all face mortality, but you can choose your actions and responses until then.

I remember when my mother was first diagnosed with cancer. She hadn't been to the doctor regularly, and as she began going for checkups, she was advised on various procedures. This eventually led her to get a colonoscopy that she had been putting off. During the colonoscopy, the doctor found a growth and initially didn't think it was anything to worry about. Just to be sure, he took a sample and sent it off for testing. A couple of days later, the doctor called with the results. "Everything was normal except for a few cells. It doesn't look like a problem, but it is best to get it removed." And he referred her to a surgeon for removal.

The surgeon removed the growth along with the surrounding tissue and lymph nodes, stating afterward that "everything looks good" to the naked eye. A few days later, he returned and reported that her pathology reports showed the cancer had actually spread, so he would refer her to a cancer specialist to start treatment right away.

By the end of this experience, she had gone from thinking she was healthy, since she hadn't visited a doctor in a while, to discovering she had stage four cancer.

At this point, we get into the themes of power and control. She had no control over her diagnosis, the inevitability of how it developed, or the progression of the disease. She didn't even have much control over the treatments themselves, except for her choice regarding whether to undergo them. That was where she could regain some control: she could choose either to go through with the treatment or to decline it.

During our conversation, she was very emotional. Aside from this diagnosis, her father had just died, and she had recently welcomed her first grandchild. She also had a sister who had gone through chemotherapy a few years earlier, which had been so ineffective that the cancer kept returning, leading to a bone marrow transplant and eventually a loss of life. Because of all this experience, my mother perceived chemotherapy as something that would be awful and inevitable, which led her to decide that it wasn't a choice she wanted to make.

I tried to discuss all of this with her and reminded her that she had a choice. I told my mother that I would respect her choices and support whatever decisions she made. However,

I also expressed my disagreement with her choice. Because we have a strong relationship, we were able to discuss it openly.

I was very honest with her. At that time, she had just welcomed a new grandchild. This was important to her because she said to me, "I don't want my grandkids to see me going through all that pain."

I acknowledged her feelings and responded with all the experience and knowledge I had. I said, "I completely understand where you're coming from. While I'll support you, you need to realize that the choice you're making means you either won't see your grandkids grow up or you will, depending on how you approach it."

I explained that she could opt for treatment, which might slow things down. We could take things one day, one week, one month at a time and reassess the situation. Alternatively, she could decide to give up without trying, knowing that everything had progressed to a point where she might only have a couple of months left. I reminded her that her new grandchild would grow up without her if she chose that option.

Ultimately, after reflecting on it, she changed her mind, and things did not turn out as she had feared. She avoided the self-fulfilling prophecy that often accompanies such decisions. We stayed proactive, and she underwent chemotherapy, even though she disliked the experience.

A couple of years later, the cancer was gone. She went from having one grandchild to six, all because she focused on her choices rather than on the fear created by the negative experiences she had witnessed throughout her life. She learned to accept that she had a choice and would need to accept the outcomes of her decisions. In this case, she chose to undergo treatment.

Acceptance allows you to conserve your energy and avoid the frustration of trying to control the uncontrollable. It enables you to approach challenges with a sense of calm and adaptability, knowing that you can choose how you respond. Acceptance allows you to realize your true power. Acceptance allows you to stop looking outward for influence and start building true power from within. Accepting yourself allows you to set boundaries. Boundaries will give you the self-acceptance and self-confidence you need to choose your mindset and actions.

For example, you cannot control others' actions, but you can choose how to interact with them. You cannot control if someone approaches you with an angry tone about a concern they have, but you can choose whether to match their negative energy or deflect it. You cannot control the weather, but you can choose how you plan your day around it. You can't control whether it will rain, but you can choose whether you will bring an umbrella or simply dance in the puddles. By accepting what is outside of your control, you free yourself to focus on the areas where you can make a real difference.

Letting Go of Perfectionism

Perfectionism often stems from the desire to control everything, and it can be a significant source of stress and frustration. The pursuit of perfection can prevent us from taking action because we're afraid of making mistakes or of not meeting our impossibly high standards. Perfectionism is so focused on making the perfect choice that it often fails to allow any choice at all. Life isn't about being perfect and already knowing everything; it's about learning and growth. You can't learn if you never make a mistake.

True power lies in the ability to take imperfect action, to embrace mistakes as opportunities for growth, and to let go of the need for everything to be flawless. When we stop striving for perfection, we create space for creativity, progress, and resilience. Why do politicians have to run for re-election after a few years? So we can see how someone does and learn from our mistakes.

By releasing the need to control every outcome and accepting that imperfection is a natural part of life, we allow ourselves to move forward with confidence and clarity. We allow ourselves to learn and grow. We allow ourselves to let go of the fear of failure and find comfort in the journey of life. We allow ourselves to gain the true power we have had all along.

Learning to Adapt

Life is unpredictable. Situations and people change, and circumstances evolve. One of the greatest forms of control we can have is the ability to adapt to new situations with flexibility and an open mind. Accepting this allows us to focus on the internal power we possess. It will also allow us to control how we interact with others and adapt to our environment.

Being adaptable enables us to navigate challenges with creativity and innovation. Having the ability to flex our plans to focus on long-term goals helps ensure a journey to success that aligns with our goals and values.

The unexpected will happen. When it does, it will be important to adapt in a way that best fits you. Otherwise, you will be left sitting on the side of the road while life passes you by. If you can gain a new perspective and take a detour, you will eventually reach where you want and find so much more than you ever imagined along the way.

Adaptability is not weakness or compliance with changes you didn't want or agree to; it is having the strength to take something unexpected and turn it into something that still fits your plans.

Focusing on how uncertain life is can be devastating, which is why mindset is so important. A fixed mindset sees this inevitably as scary and debilitating, limiting the ability to take steps. A growth mindset recognizes that change will happen and fosters the adaptability necessary for growth and the experience of many opportunities. It allows you to make a plan while appreciating all the unplanned experiences along the way.

It's About the Journey, Not the Destination

While it's natural to focus on the destination we planned, true power comes from focusing on the journey. Think of any achievement you have reached. What means more to you: the certificate in the frame or the work it took to get there?

When we put our energy into the steps we can control, rather than obsessing over the end result, we free ourselves from the pressure of perfection and create a healthier, more sustainable approach to achieving our goals. We enjoy the experience and lessons learned in achieving the outcome more than the trophy on the mantle or the certificate on the wall.

I can remember planning a family vacation to Disney World. My wife put so much time and effort into every detail. We were going to take our girls to ride all the rides, meet all the characters, and eat all the delicacies. In May 2020, we were going to take the girls on one of the best vacations they would ever have.

I am sure you can imagine how it went just by reading the date. In March 2020, the entire world changed. You can be sure none of that was in my wife's plans. March turned to April, and April to May, as the entire world tried to navigate the COVID-19 pandemic. It took a year before we could really start planning another trip close to the original.

So much had changed at this point: character experiences were almost nonexistent and behind glass, prices were skyrocketing to cover extra cleaning and safety precautions, and indoor restaurants often required masks. In March 2022, it was finally happening… until the week before we were supposed to leave, I got sick with COVID-19. Again, the trip was pushed off until May. Those extra two months made a huge difference, though.

By adapting to the ever-changing environment around us, we eventually had one of the best family vacations. Our girls loved meeting and interacting with the characters. Because we waited two more months, they could. My daughters were able to see and interact with so many more Disney characters than if we had gone in March. Furthermore, the time saved by skipping seeing the additional characters allowed them more time for rides.

One thing we failed to plan for was how much more they would enjoy rides at this stage. We were even able to complete the "mountain challenge" by riding all the mountain-themed coasters in one day. How you get on rides has changed. It used to be you could book them in advance, but during our trip, you had to book them by 6 a.m.

The coolest part? Disney unveiled a brand-new ride at Epcot Center two weeks ahead of our scheduled visit. By requiring us to log on and book our rides the day we went, my daughters and I were able to catch a roller coaster before almost anyone else in the world!

Focusing on the process allowed us to take consistent, intentional action without being overly attached to or deviating from the outcome. When the pandemic changed our trip to Disney World, it didn't actually change the destination, just the journey. We still went; the path was just different from what we had planned.

Focusing on the process allows you to enjoy the journey, to learn along the way, and to find fulfillment in the work itself. When we focus on the process, we also open ourselves to unexpected opportunities and outcomes that we may not have anticipated. We create a space for the unexpected to bring us something more wonderful than we ever imagined.

The Freedom of Letting Go

Now, rather than conclude this chapter on such a heavy note, let's look at another example. I want to refer back to my oldest daughter. Not only is she sure of what she can and can't do, but she is also incredibly self-confident and accepts who she is. While we've talked about how her mindset can sometimes be negative and inhibit her from trying new things, she is also very self-aware and self-confident.

I remember when she tried out for the school volleyball team; she hadn't had much training, but she still gave it a shot. As good parents, my wife and I tried to explain to her that many other kids were also trying out. We even asked her how she felt about it. She understood that not everyone would make the team, but she was so confident that she would succeed that she was completely devastated when she didn't. Now that she has grown as a volleyball player and is having much more fun with it, it's interesting to reflect on those tryouts.

When we talk to her about that experience and have similar conversations now, she looks right at us and says, "Listen, I'm out there doing my best. If they can't see that, then I don't really need to be on this team anyway." She'll also say things like, "I'm giving it my all, and this is who I am. If they can't accept me for that and don't want me on their team, that's fine; I'll just play for another team." It's refreshing to see her self-acceptance and how it helps her navigate different challenges in her life. She is a perfect example of self-acceptance and of not letting the world around you change who you are.

Ultimately, the freedom that comes from focusing on what you can control lies in letting go of the need for certainty. Letting go of the need to control every outcome allows you to live more fully in the present, to embrace change, and to make the most of every moment. Freedom comes in accepting the reality that things will change, and you can only control how you take in and respond to those changes.

When you stop trying to force life to unfold according to your plans and expectations, you allow yourself to experience a deeper sense of peace and freedom. You begin to trust yourself and the flow of life, knowing you have the strength to navigate whatever comes your way. When you start with self-assurance, you find self-confidence. With self-confidence comes peace, the ability to accept what you can and cannot control, and the freedom to live fully in the journey.

The journey will continue in the next chapter as we explore the possibilities of the detours. We will discuss the importance of recognizing alternative viewpoints and how being open to other possibilities can enrich the journey rather than derail it. Seeking other possibilities allows us to broaden our perspective through understanding, so we can use our power responsibly.

Reflection Questions

1. What situations in your life are currently causing stress because you are trying to control things that are outside your influence?
2. When unexpected changes occur, do you tend to resist, fear, or adapt to them? What does that response reveal about your mindset?
3. Which area of personal control needs the most attention in your life right now: your mindset, actions, habits, emotional responses, or boundaries? What is one practical step you can take this week to focus less on controlling outcomes and more on controlling your response, effort, and attitude?

CHAPTER 13

BE AWARE OF OTHER POSSIBILITIES

Too much focus on power and control can turn into a fixed mindset and prevent us from achieving the very thing we are seeking.

Focusing on one thing creates a narrowed view. Peripheral vision is necessary to see the broader picture. This is the difference between a fixed and a growth mindset. With a fixed mindset, we are so focused on one particular thing, such as a goal, plan, or desire, that we lose sight of the things around us and become unprepared for life's uncertainties. A growth mindset gives us peripheral vision; we can see changes coming and adapt to them. A fixed mindset significantly limits us: our power, our choices, our relationships, and our influence.

This chapter explores ways to expand our thinking and build relationships, fostering a growth mindset rather than a fixed one. Having a growth mindset will set the tone for accepting and dissecting new information for new opportunities. It will allow us to adapt and experience so many things.

However, this can be quite challenging. It's difficult to confront our deeply ingrained beliefs, which are often shaped by our upbringing. While it's not always necessary to change these beliefs, it is crucial to challenge ourselves to ensure that, in conversations, we aren't using them to filter our interpretation of information. Instead, we should create open avenues for others around us to express their views.

Conversations must be two-way interactions. Challenging our beliefs doesn't mean changing them. When we can have open and honest conversations, challenging our beliefs can also strengthen them.

This concept ties back to our understanding of power. We've discussed the power of choice and that true power lies within us. Additionally, we possess the power of curiosity. This curiosity allows us to form bonds and build relationships with others.

While conviction and clarity are important, they can also narrow our focus and limit our potential. When we become too rigid in our thinking, we may miss opportunities for growth, new insights, and creative solutions. True power lies not only in knowing where we stand but also in being open to the vast range of possibilities that exist beyond our current perspective.

We started the book by outlining how our reality isn't always *the* reality. Our reality is shaped by our perceptions of the situation. Our perceptions are shaped by our experiences and beliefs.

This chapter is about the power of having different perspectives: considering and embracing alternative viewpoints. We do this by intentionally seeking out other angles and being open to learning. Having other perspectives can help us solidify what we already know or look for something new. Either way is growth: either growth in our confidence in our current perspective or growth in discovering something new.

Being Fixed by a Fixed Mindset

Each of our journeys is unique. We each have different experiences that provide us a different perspective on the world. Upbringing, education, beliefs, values, relationships, and so many other aspects of life vary from person to person. Our life journey shapes the lens through which we view the world and, in turn, our perceptions.

Recognizing only our own journey creates a fixed mindset and stunts growth. Without acknowledging other perspectives, we ignore others. Staying in a fixed mindset closes us off from the world and limits how we can navigate the detours we encounter along the way.

I see these issues a lot in parenting my children. I have goals for how I want to parent and what I want them to become. These ideas have come from various aspects of my life experiences. I have learned, however, that I can't parent both of them the same way. Despite growing up in the same house with the same parents, they are vastly different. They have different wants and needs. Having a fixed parenting style that doesn't adapt to each child's wants and needs fails everyone: me, my wife, and my kids.

Sometimes the same style works in different ways; other times, a new approach is needed. Luckily, I didn't have to go through much of a tantrum phase with my kids. My oldest daughter threw herself down once when she was around two. She lightly hit her head on the floor, and her face instantly showed a look of, "That hurt. Why did I think this was a good idea?" She never threw a fit again.

My youngest daughter did the same thing with almost the same response. The difference was that she threw a fit a few more times. The first time, she got mad at the floor for impeding her progress. The next two times, she would pause her tantrum, gently lie on the floor, then resume. After she realized she wasn't getting any response, she just stopped. My oldest daughter just needed us to let her try. My youngest daughter needed us to ignore her plea for attention. Same style, same result, different journeys to get there.

There have also been plenty of times when a different approach was needed. They have different wants, likes, and motivations. I saw this when teaching them to ride a bicycle. My oldest daughter didn't really care if she had training wheels or not. Offering her a brand-new bicycle for riding without training wheels wasn't a great motivator. I had to be more direct and intentional with her, offering encouragement. She caught on quickly and never looked back.

My youngest daughter required little encouragement. Her older sister didn't have training wheels, so she didn't want them. She told us she would get a new bicycle once her training wheels came off, because that is how it worked in her mind.

I did, however, have to take a different approach. While my oldest daughter simply needed help with the mechanics of riding a bicycle without training wheels, my youngest needed coaching through a range of emotions. She needed more time to talk about it and more encouragement that she was on the right path and wasn't taking too long. In the end, both learned to ride their bicycles, but each had a different journey to get there. Different journeys mean I had to adapt and find a different perspective.

We see this a lot in industry. Some employees are motivated by paychecks and respond to raises and bonuses. Others want to have a say in how things are done and respond more positively to opportunities to participate in groups that offer feedback or create new ideas. Others value personal performance and respond to recognition or awards. Leaders have to adapt their style to get the most out of everyone. A leader who is too rigid and stuck in a fixed mindset of how they want to do things will cause a disconnection with others, leading to dissatisfaction and turnover.

Looking beyond your personal perspective gives you a more complete view. This leads to better problem-solving, more ideas, and avenues for influence and change. Seeking different views requires a growth mindset and an openness to new possibilities. The more open you are to understanding others, the more you foster connections. The more connections you make, the more effective you become in finding solutions that benefit everyone or create common ground.

The Role of Empathy in Expanding Possibilities

Empathy is one of the most powerful tools we have for understanding other perspectives. Empathy is often confused with sympathy, yet they have vastly different definitions. Sympathy is telling someone you have been where they are. While this may seem kind, it often triggers a negative response.

Remember those experiences and perceptions? Even if your friend is going through the death of a parent and you have been through the exact same thing, you still cannot completely relate to or sympathize with it. Your relationship with your parents was different.

Conversely, empathy allows you to sit with them, which triggers a positive response and helps build a relationship. When we empathize with others, we step into their shoes and try to see the world through their eyes. This doesn't mean agreeing with everything they believe, but it does mean acknowledging their feelings, experiences, and viewpoints. When your friend suffers the loss of a parent, simply sitting with them and listening, showing empathy, will provide more comfort than saying you know exactly how they feel.

By practicing empathy, we can break down the barriers that separate us from others and create space for collaboration, compromise, and growth. Empathy opens the door to new possibilities by fostering deeper understanding and connection. Understanding and connection lead to relationships. Relationships lead to the power of influence.

For example, when we listen to others without judgment or the desire to "win" an argument, we create an environment where diverse ideas can flourish. This openness allows us to consider solutions we might never have thought of on our own. We begin to see new perspectives, which allow us to challenge ourselves. Challenge promotes growth and self-acceptance.

The Importance of Challenging Your Beliefs

One of the most powerful ways to expand your perspective is by actively challenging your beliefs. It's natural to hold on to the ideas that feel most comfortable and familiar, but personal growth and true power come from questioning those beliefs and seeking alternative viewpoints. If you don't agree with a new view, it will, in turn, solidify your current beliefs and help you to be more self-aware and self-assured.

Challenging your beliefs doesn't mean abandoning your values or becoming wishy-washy. It means being willing to question your assumptions, learn from others, and be open to change. When you challenge your beliefs, you create space for growth and transformation. You also become more adaptable and resilient in the face of new information or changing circumstances. Being adaptable and flexible is key to accepting things beyond your control, which helps you gain control of your internal power.

For example, if you believe that success can only be achieved through hard work and sacrifice, you might find yourself missing out on opportunities for rest, balance, or creativity. But if you challenge that belief and consider alternative possibilities, you might discover that success can also be nurtured through collaboration, play, and innovation. While "success" does require hard work, only focusing on a career leads you to miss out on many other "successful" areas of life, such as marriage, kids, and friends.

By challenging your beliefs, you allow yourself to evolve and grow with life's ever-changing landscape. Challenge doesn't necessarily mean change. Sometimes, challenge means validation. Challenging your beliefs and upholding them makes them stronger. Finding out which parts aren't currently relevant allows you to grow and adapt.

Either way, you allow yourself to enjoy life and create opportunities for growth that you might not otherwise have. You discover who you truly are and learn to carry self-assurance along your journey of life.

Challenge Through Curiosity

Curiosity is a powerful tool. Approaching life with a curious attitude means constantly seeking to learn, explore, and understand. Curiosity leads to questioning. Questioning leads to answers. Answers bring information and different perspectives.

Keeping the status quo means having a fixed mindset. Being curious and asking questions fosters a growth mindset. The more questions you ask, the more you learn. The more you learn, the more possibilities you have.

Having more possibilities doesn't just mean adopting different views. Asking questions helps foster connection and build relationships. Questioning leads to collaboration, more creative solutions to problems, and more opportunities for growth. It creates an environment of openness and encouragement. Being able to safely question things opens conversations and helps provide understanding.

An open mindset enables us to respond with more grace and compassion. We may not agree with everyone, but we can find common ground and understand differing viewpoints. Understanding does not require agreement; rather, it fosters respect. When we respect others, we show compassion, which helps us build stronger relationships. These relationships, in turn, empower us to influence those around us.

We often observe the power of curiosity in children. Interestingly, the same behaviors we notice in kids also appear in the professional world. What is it that kids always ask? "Why?" We can carry this curiosity into the workplace as well.

One effective problem-solving method is known as the "Five Whys." This technique encourages you to ask "why" five times to uncover the root cause of an issue. For example, if someone trips and falls while walking down the hall, you might ask:

Why did they fall?

Because they were on their phone.

Why were they on their phone?

Because they were trying to text their boss to let them know they were on their way.

Why were they texting their boss?

Because they were rushing from one meeting to another, with one meeting ending at 1 p.m. and the next starting at 1 p.m.

Why were those meetings scheduled that way?

Because that's how the meeting times were arranged.

By following this cadence, you can gradually identify the root cause of the problem. In this case, it might lead to the suggestion that meetings should last only 50 minutes rather than an hour to help prevent such issues in the future.

I remember a personal experience with my youngest daughter when she was about two years old. As my wife was putting our daughter to bed one night, she expressed her frustration about always feeling second. She was tired of it, and this feeling was understandably upsetting for her.

She's the youngest in our family. Her birthday is later in the year, so when we look at the calendar from January to December, her sister gets to celebrate her birthday before she does. She is frustrated about being second and wants to understand why this always happens. Before bed, she expresses her frustration through a conversation with my wife.

The cycle of questions starts: "Why am I always second?"

To this, my wife replies, "Well, honey, I don't really know. That's just how you were made."

Then my daughter asks, "Why was I made that way?"

"That's just kind of how you came."

"Well, why did I come out that way?"

"That's how God made you."

To this, my daughter asks, "Well, why did He make me that way?"

"I don't know," my wife says. "You'll have to take that up with Him."

My daughter's response? "Oh, I will." Then she rolls over and goes to sleep.

This exchange illustrates how asking "why" helps us foster relationships and gain new perspectives that enhance our lives. It aids in our growth, allowing us to influence the world around us rather than simply being influenced by it. This helps us gain control over our reactions, and that's where our true power lies.

Avoiding the Trap of Bias

Earlier, we discussed some of the common forms of bias. It is worth noting that "bias" is being used in its simplest sense: biases are human tendencies to gravitate toward or react in certain ways. Our biases are more than how we treat other people. They are the heart of how we unconsciously and unintentionally seek and interpret information. Our biases will have us naturally gravitate toward information that supports our current view rather than challenge it.

As we discussed, challenging doesn't mean changing. We also need to challenge our views to solidify them and gain self-assurance. Without intentionally seeking out new perspectives, we live in our biases. In an age where data is abundant and technology is in nearly every aspect of life, the problem is even more apparent. Algorithms and artificial intelligence analyze our clicks, likes, and posts for trends, revealing our biases. This information is used to serve ads, pop-ups, and posts that reflect our identified interests. Without pausing to accept this and intentionally looking to verify our views through other sources, we fall into the trap of living through our biases. Such behavior prevents us from taking control over our perceptions and having the power to form meaningful connections and relationships.

You see this every day while scrolling through social media. You decided you are in the market for a new blender and looked up some reviews online. Minutes later, as you are scrolling through your favorite social media platform, there is a blender in every ad. Take a brain break on a game, and you have more ads for blenders.

The same is true when it comes to views. Someone tells you about a world event. Algorithms and artificial intelligence will pick up on the headlines you click on and show you more news from that view. A specific example is a war in another country. Which headline do you click to find your information? *"Rebels have seized the capital, causing the current leader to go into hiding,"* or *"Activists have reclaimed the capital after the leader fled to escape captivity."*

The answer will determine the lean you have toward a view and the information you will continue to receive. Clicking the first leans toward supporting the current regime, while the latter leans toward supporting the people's efforts. In one, the people are "rebels" simply fighting the system, while in the other, the people are "activists" seeking fair and equitable solutions for all. Without consciously choosing both sides, you will only ever see one.

Collaboration for Diverse Perspectives

Collaboration is about more than simply working together. It provides new ideas, fresh perspectives, and creative solutions. Having different views of the same problem leads to possibilities that wouldn't otherwise exist. Simply talking through problems with someone adds new ideas and information that can lead to better solutions.

Most likely, you can think of a time you were talking to someone about a problem you were having, and they offered a solution that helped. You probably even thought: *Why didn't I think of that!?* While this question is often rhetorical, the answer is quite simple: you didn't think of it because the person who did had a different perspective.

As a leader, I often see this with new employees, especially those with industry experience. When interacting with new employees, I make a point of drawing out any past experiences they have that relate to their new roles. While this is mainly to help them feel more comfortable, it often creates an avenue for new ideas simply because they bring a different perspective. Through these conversations, I have seen relationships form that allow institutions to introduce changes to current practice or capitalize on employees' strengths simply because someone had a different perspective to offer.

Diversity is a common theme in today's work environment. Anyone employed by a company has likely heard how our differences make us more efficient. While it is true that having different perspectives can lead to more creative solutions through diverse skills and experiences, the same is true in life. By embracing differences in your daily life, you foster dialogue with others and build the relationships necessary for growth.

I am sure that if you look at the people around you in your personal life, they all have different skills. Even if you are lifelong friends and your lives seem incredibly similar, it is very likely that each of you has something different to add that makes the group stronger as a whole.

You are probably already identifying the planner, the risk taker, the thinker, and the wallflower. Almost every group has that one person who will always make the plan for everyone to get together, the person who is always up for a new experience, the one who needs to analyze if the venue has enough lighting and a good menu, and the person who probably wouldn't even go anywhere if not for the friendship of this group.

Accepting the Unexpected

Finding new perspectives is about more than developing relationships with people; it is also about your relationship with uncertainty. Life is rarely black and white, and it is full of unpredictable twists and turns. Each one brings new opportunities and experiences. The way we relate to these unplanned events will determine our experiences. If the unexpected creates fear, anxiety, and frustration, we are stuck in the cycle of the fixed mindset. If life's changes bring new adventures and opportunities, we are living with a growth mindset, seeking new perspectives.

Uncertainty should bring curiosity, not fear. The unexpected is an opportunity to explore, learn, and grow. It is a reminder that control lies solely within ourselves and is expressed through our actions. The unexpected didn't happen because we didn't plan well enough or because we didn't have enough control. It is a reminder that we need to try something new. We need to seek a different angle and be open to learning from these detours on our journey through life.

Uncertainty is an opportunity to embrace a growth mindset and practice flexibility and adaptability. Letting go of the rigidity of a fixed mindset opens the door to freedom, creativity, and innovation. Changes to the route don't typically change the destination, just the ride along the way.

I felt this going through nursing school. It took me longer than it should have to become a nurse. However, this led to opportunities I would never have had. These experiences had a ripple effect I never could have imagined. If I had followed my plan, I would have simply gone to one school, completed my degree, and gone to work. Life had other plans.

Through the frustrating experiences of attending different programs, starting over, and overcoming all sorts of other obstacles, I discovered many experiences and relationships I would not have otherwise had. One of my best friends in life today comes from a nursing program I didn't finish. I was able to travel to Bolivia to provide medical care in remote villages, which has given me a perspective I never would have dreamed of. Taking so many electives to meet different program requirements allowed me to study many aspects of life.

In the end, I still became a nurse. The difference is that the journey to get there wasn't the one I originally planned. Instead, it was something so much more than I could imagine. I never would have experienced all of that without embracing these uncertainties in some capacity.

Accepting that life will bring unexpected changes helps us embrace them as they come. Embracing uncertainty is essential. If we remain unaware that uncertainty will arise and that there are multiple possibilities, we risk falling into a cycle of disappointment and frustration when things don't go our way. We must remember that our reality is not the only one; everyone navigates their own unique experiences. Not everyone will be able to adapt to changes. Everyone has the power to, but not everyone will accept it.

In the next chapter, we'll discuss how to balance our understanding of perception and power to foster greater harmony and more effective leadership in our lives.

Reflection Questions

1. Where in your life are you most likely to approach situations with a fixed mindset rather than with curiosity and openness to other possibilities?
2. Think about a time when another person's perspective helped you solve a problem, understand a situation more clearly, or grow in an unexpected way. What did that experience teach you?
3. What is one practical way you can become more intentional this week about seeking another viewpoint, asking better questions, or staying open to an unexpected detour?

CHAPTER 14

USE PERCEPTION TO PUT POWER BACK INTO BALANCE

Now let's explore how we can use perception to restore balance to power, as they often feed off each other.

This concept resembles a dance. When we dance with a partner, balance is crucial. If one person moves to the left while the other moves to the right, or if one person leaps into the air without the other being ready to catch them, it can create an imbalance that wreaks havoc and causes damage. This scenario involves physical harm, but in our lives, we also encounter emotional and intellectual harm. Therefore, it's essential to achieve emotional regulation.

We have discussed in detail how perception is shaped by our experiences and leads to our actions. Controlling our perceptions gives us the power to control our actions and influence the world around us. Power can be overwhelming and magnificent. Having a balance of perception and power will determine if you use power responsibly or fall into the trap of the chase. Just as power is internal, so too is gaining and mastering it. It takes control of oneself to both achieve and use power responsibly.

This chapter will aim to give you that balance. By harnessing perception, you gain power. Through control of self, you can grow and use it. When the forces of power and perception are balanced, they become renewable. The more balanced they are, the more power you have.

Balancing the Tightrope Act

We have already shown how intertwined perception and power are. They are so in sync that one almost doesn't exist without the other. Without the right perception, we fail to gain power outside of our illusions of control. Power without the right perception is nothing more than a fleeting, superficial source.

The same is true for breaking this cycle. Accepting power as an internal rather than an external force leads to the ability to shape perception, opening up a whole new world of powerful possibilities.

All of this starts with self-recognition of what shapes your personal lens to view the world. Next comes acceptance, both of self and new ideas. Accepting your unique perspectives, experiences, and opinions will help you begin to seek other views, transforming self-acceptance into self-confidence while also building relationships. Accepting that your reality isn't *the* reality and having a new understanding of the definition of power becomes a wonderful cycle of renewable power, new opportunities, creative solutions, and influence.

Almost any circus has tightrope walkers. After flying through the air on trapezes, the performers move to platforms high above the ground. The nets are removed in dramatic fashion, and only a small rope remains for the performers to walk from platform to platform. After daringly crossing to the other side, objects are added to distract the performers as they venture back. Long sticks, items to juggle, and even flames all attempt to knock them off balance, but the performers always prevail.

The same is true for all of us in life. We constantly try to stay on the narrow path of schedules, family, work, and fun. Along the way, there are distractions from technology, sickness, politics, and almost anything happening in our current world. Just as the performers were able to juggle everything and stay on their rope with practice, we can, too, in everyday life. The more we practice accepting ourselves, regulating our exposure to distractions, and pausing to reflect, the more we will be able to stay on our path. Achieving a balance of power and perception takes awareness and practice.

The Role of Emotional Intelligence in Balance

One of the most crucial components of balancing perception and power is emotional intelligence. Emotional intelligence involves the ability to recognize, understand, and manage our emotions, as well as the ability to recognize, understand, and influence the emotions of others. Sound familiar? It should. This has been the theme of the entire book.

Having emotional intelligence means being aware of your own emotions. This helps you to pause and self-reflect. When you do, you can learn and build relationships with others. Relationships allow you to influence the world around you.

When we cultivate emotional intelligence, we can navigate the complexities of power more effectively. For example, when we encounter resistance or conflict, emotional intelligence allows us to perceive the underlying emotions and motivations at play, giving us insight on how to respond with empathy and clarity. Instead of reacting impulsively or defensively, we can choose a measured response that preserves relationships and encourages constructive dialogue.

Emotional intelligence also helps us stay grounded in the face of power. When we are in positions of influence or authority, it's easy to become disconnected from the feelings and needs of others. It keeps us aware of the emotions of others and encourages us to exert compassion and humility. By empathizing with others, we develop relationships, fostering connection and collaboration.

Authentic and meaningful relationships are important because they provide a trusted source to help keep our perceptions and actions balanced. This ensures that we don't misuse our power to manipulate or control others but instead use it to uplift and inspire.

The Mirror of Self-Reflection

If self-recognition and acceptance are the starting point of the journey, self-reflection is the key to sustainability. Things change and need to be constantly evaluated. Any successful industry will evaluate a process change after it occurs to determine whether it was effective and whether it needs to be improved or replaced to maximize efficiency. This is what self-reflection does for us in life. Self-reflection should be a consistent practice to ensure our perceptions are balanced and don't need adjustment or replacement.

Previously, we learned the importance of looking at life through the right lens. The same is true when reflecting on your inner self. And just like the lens shaping your perceptions of the external is important, so is using the correct mirror for self-reflection.

Most carnivals still have a funhouse. Within almost every funhouse is a hall of mirrors. Each has a slightly different curve, finish, or shape, offering different views of ourselves. In one, we have a huge forehead; in another, we are super tall; and in another, we are really short. Choosing the right mirror is important for ensuring self-reflection. Getting the right mirror for self-reflection relies on openness to learning, actively seeking the views of others, and being humble. When practicing self-reflection on a regular basis, we gain insight and control.

The balance we seek comes from having a "pause moment": being self-aware enough to recognize our emotions, experiences, and biases and being able to pause long enough to listen to others and build relationships. This pause comes from regular self-reflection. Being able to pause and interpret our internal feelings allows us to gain control over our external actions.

Pausing for reflection helps us maintain control over what we can control and how to use our power responsibly. Taking time for self-reflection enables us to consider how our perceptions are shaping our use of power. Are we perceiving situations through a lens of scarcity, competition, or judgment? Are we using power to control others or to empower them? The answer to this question can help us determine if we are operating with a fixed or growth mindset.

Like anything else, self-reflection takes practice. It starts with a lot of intentionality, humility, and grace. Over time, it becomes a habit. Pretty soon, self-reflection becomes a daily practice, and power is renewed by the ability to consistently pause and take in new information. Feedback becomes a gift, and growth becomes exponential. The habit of consistent self-reflection keeps perception and power in balance.

Responsible Accountability

While responsibility and accountability are inherently different, they go hand in hand. If power is to be exercised responsibly, accountability must follow. Earlier, we discussed how power must be used in a responsible way with consideration for the consequences. Accountability is accepting and adapting to those consequences. This requires integrity and humility: integrity to use power responsibly, with consideration of how it will impact others; humility to recognize when power is misused or misses the mark, and to accept the information for future consideration.

Almost everyone has heard at some point, "It's not what you said; it's how you said it." This speaks to the importance of nonverbal communication. What this also means is there are times when we have the best intentions with communicating or receiving a message, but someone else has a completely different interpretation and response.

Read this sentence: *"How are you doing?"* This seems harmless, but small changes in tone and situation can drastically change how this message is perceived. Ask someone this question while passing each other in the hall, and you will get a "fine" and move on with your day. Ask someone this question after losing a loved one or hearing a devastating diagnosis, and the reaction is much different. Ask the question with emphasis on the word "you," and it almost seems accusatory. Ask it with a New York-Italian accent, and it instills laughter, thanks to a popular sitcom. To use power responsibly means being able to take accountability for the consequences, good and bad.

Accountability and Integrity

While responsibility and accountability go together like peanut butter and jelly, you can't have either without integrity, just like you can't make a peanut butter and jelly sandwich without bread. In either case, you need a base to work with. Integrity serves as the basis for how we use power and accept its consequences. Integrity is our ability to set our own boundaries and determine what actions are acceptable and which aren't.

Our foundational values and beliefs shape the integrity we uphold. They determine which actions we deem acceptable and which are a line not to be crossed. Integrity determines the action, and actions require responsibility and accountability.

Pretend someone came to you and said your best friend is about to lose their job, but you can't say anything. This person confided in you because they needed someone to share their feelings with. They are afraid of their own job stability because if your bestie isn't safe, then who is?

Your response to this situation is based on your integrity. If your integrity lies in loyalty and emotions, you will likely run to the friend and tell them about the impending news, despite being specifically asked not to. Your integrity dictates that loyalty to your friend is your highest priority.

On the other hand, you may choose to respect the decision and not say anything. Your best friend is still your best friend, so you aren't idle. You plan and prepare. You figure out things to say and resources to offer. You plan drinks at the end of the day, after you know it is going to happen, so you can be supportive. In this instance, your integrity lies in mutual trust and understanding. While not saying anything is difficult, building mutual trust with others establishes a boundary that prevents you from saying anything to your friend.

In this situation, neither response is inherently wrong, just different. The reason there are different responses is that people have different understandings of integrity. For some, it is perfectly acceptable to share secret knowledge as long as it is perceived to do good. In this scenario, integrity allows you to break a coworker's trust for the greater good of a perceived stronger relationship with your best friend.

Others have a different perception. If you feel secrets are not to be shared and your relationship with your friend would be more strengthened by helping them through this difficult time, you take another approach. In this case, you prepare to be there for your friend and anticipate their needs, but you let the proper authorities bear the bad news of a job loss. After all, how do you really know your friend will inevitably lose their job? Things change, and not all information is accurate.

Integrity sets the foundation for your actions, but actions have consequences. Telling your friend seems like a great idea, but it, too, has consequences. You broke your coworker's trust, and if something changes or the information is wrong, you may break your friend's trust by giving them false information and inciting such negative emotion.

Not telling your friend has its own set of consequences. If they find out you knew and didn't tell them, that may break trust. Integrity determines the path, responsibility empowers action, and accountability accepts consequences.

Staying Humble

Humility helps to counterbalance the difficulty of actions. I described the scenario above with a purpose. It likely seemed to most of you that there wasn't a great solution. You may even have noticed that, in both situations, I proposed a fractured friendship and mistrust as a consequence. Humility helps you recognize the difficulty of the situation and allows you to accept the consequences with grace. Humility allows for understanding and growth.

In the scenario above, you had no control over being placed in the situation. Unless you have a time machine, you can't unhear something. You didn't ask your coworker to tell you; they just did. The only control you had was in your actions following the conversation.

Earlier, I mentioned how we always have a choice. We may not like it, but we have one. This concept is evident in this scenario, and humility is what will get you through. Integrity will determine which choice you make, and responsibility will allow you to act on that choice. Each choice has consequences. Taking accountability sounds easy until it comes at the cost of hurting a relationship with your best friend over a situation you never asked to be part of. Humility allows you to recognize that you did the best you could and to give yourself grace to grieve and grow.

Externally, humility is a bit different. Humility with others might look like giving credit for contributions, admitting when we don't know something, or actively and openly seeking feedback to improve. By embracing humility, we maintain a sense of balance, preventing the abuse or corruption of power and ensuring that we remain connected to our values and the needs of those around us. Embracing humility is about acknowledging that we'll never be perfect. The good news is that some of the most successful people learn from their mistakes, which is how we grow.

I have worked with a lot of people and have noticed something about high performers: they seem to learn a lot more from their mistakes than from being shown how to do something. Think about a time in life when you needed to learn something. Maybe it was a new work computer system or a new device at home. You read the manual and try to do some research. What ultimately works best? Having someone show you can help you understand what you're learning, but what usually does the trick for many people is making a mistake and figuring out how to fix it.

When you make a mistake, you feel uncomfortable. Once you have to humble yourself to ask for help and fumble through figuring it out, you don't want that feeling to come back. It becomes a motivator to prevent the mistake from happening again. If you read the manuals, why did you even make the mistake? Because the manuals can't replicate that uncomfortable feeling that successfully motivated your brain to begin retaining information.

Have you ever accidentally sent a text to the wrong person? You were shown how to text and even read social media clickbait about people who accidentally texted the wrong person. We see all kinds of clickbait promising hilarity at the expense of people who have awkwardly texted the wrong person. After sending *"I love you"* to your boss instead of your spouse, you likely learned a valuable lesson. You probably started putting safeguards in place, like double-checking the name on the thread before hitting send or reserving some conversations for in-person discussions. Moving on required humility and adaptation.

Humility takes practice, and it comes from self-reflection. Nobody is perfect. Having a clear view of the consequences of our actions will help promote the humility we need to learn and grow. When we do this, we can accept ourselves for who we are, imperfections and all.

Acceptance is not just about the world around us but about recognizing and embracing our identity. Self-acceptance is just the first step of the journey. To continue, we must have integrity to guide decisions, responsibility to act on them, accountability to accept the consequences, and humility to accept them with grace, which will help us balance our lives.

Giving to Receive

Throughout this book, we've discussed the difference between good and bad cycles. By now, you hopefully have some tools and understanding to help break the bad cycles and enter into the good ones. Gaining new perspectives and practicing responsible use of power are gifts. While we shouldn't give simply to receive, seeking out other perspectives and taking control of our actions becomes a cycle of renewable power. Every time we give, we receive.

Being intentional cultivates relationships that empower everyone involved. Intentionality breaks the cycle of the power chase and creates an entirely new one that feeds itself. It takes self-awareness to be intentional. Intentionality leads to relationships. Having integrity determines choice, responsibility allows action, and accountability accepts consequences. Regular self-reflection through a humble mirror allows for processing, acceptance, and the cycle to begin again.

This cycle is so contrary to that of modern society. Being able to actively seek other perspectives, when so many are content to be stuck in their own fixed view, is so different that people will notice. Relationships will form and have ripple effects, often bigger than you can ever imagine or plan.

Even better, these relationships become self-sustaining, providing even more freedom and power. When you listen to others, they feel heard. When they feel heard, they connect. Where connection exists, there is influence. Influence means the power to keep learning and growing.

The power of living with intention and fostering connection will return even more power than we put into it. Where we start with the power to connect, we gain the power to influence, the power of creativity, and the power to create positive change.

The winter holidays bring a time of celebration. Not everyone celebrates the same way or recognizes the same holidays, but almost everyone spends time with family and friends, and gift-giving is likely involved. One of the best traditions of the season is giving gifts to kids. Their reactions are unpredictable and honest. A toy that costs less than $5 can be received as the best gift on the planet, or a pair of shoes may seem like one of the worst. Either way, kids will show appreciation in their own way.

If we never know what response to expect, why do we keep giving gifts? Because we feel joy in their appreciation. The same is true in life. Life is naturally cyclical: we are born, we live, we die, and the cycle repeats. The good news with the cycles of perception and power is that you get to choose; you can either live in the chaos from the cycle of the power chase, or you can choose to take the nearest exit ramp and enjoy the possibilities from the cycle of new perspectives, connection, and relationship.

You now have a formula you can use to begin taking control of your perception and wield your power responsibly. This process can lead to so many more possibilities. Focusing on the self brings the ability to connect and create positive change in our lives and communities.

Reflection Questions

1. How could regular self-reflection help you recognize when your perceptions, emotions, or actions need to be adjusted?
2. Think about a recent situation where integrity, responsibility, accountability, and humility all played a role in your response. What did that experience teach you about balance?
3. What is one practical habit you can begin this week to help keep perception and power in balance, such as pausing before reacting, seeking feedback, or reflecting on the consequences of your actions?

CONCLUSION

This is the end of our long journey down the road of finding power in perception. What began with being aware of how our reality isn't *the* reality has offered an upside-down view of where power truly lies. The first step on this journey was self-awareness, but that was just the beginning. Along the way were self-confidence, relationships, connection, and collaboration. This led to integrity, responsibility, and accountability. Finally, humility allowed it all to start over again.

It's essential to remember that self-awareness and self-reflection are incredibly powerful. When you reach a point where you can accept yourself for who you truly are, you'll be able to take those moments to pause and genuinely listen to others and build meaningful relationships. This acceptance will put you on the right path.

Here are some steps you can take to get there:

The GPS on the Perception Journey

1. Start with **self-awareness**: Be aware of who you are, including your thoughts, beliefs, experiences, biases, and the factors that shape how you interpret and respond to your surroundings.
2. Turn right into **self-acceptance**: Accept the person you are. Giving yourself patience, grace, and understanding allows you to give the same to others.

3. Take the on-ramp to **self-reflection**: Embrace the power to pause. Being able to pause and reflect before responding gives you power over your reactions.
4. **Self-learning** reported ahead: Being open to learning allows you to grow. When you learn from others, you connect with them and form relationships. Having relationships gives you the power to influence the world around you through your actions.
5. When you see **self-responsibility**, you have reached your destination: Use your power wisely. Relationships should not be used to manipulate others to meet a hidden agenda. Influence should come in the form of connection, not coercion. Accept consequences and humbly allow yourself grace.

Life is a journey. On any journey, it is helpful to have some direction. Although there will be detours along the way, our perceptions can help us navigate these situations. Hopefully, by now, you have at least a little different perspective than you had before. You can agree or disagree, and you may not make any immediate changes, but just reaching this part of the journey should have brought growth.

Just like with any journey, perception isn't passive. Actively seeking new information and vantage points requires intentionality, and it all starts with self-awareness. Once you get into the routine, it is important to stay diligent, just like you have to watch the road even when the car is in cruise control. Consistently practicing self-reflection keeps you diligent on your journey and open to new adventures.

Having different perceptions adds to the journey of life, just the way different sites add to the experience of a vacation. Very few people I know go on vacation and simply sit in the hotel room all day. Even when staying in a resort, there is an array of experiences: dinner, pools, time together, etc. In life, we need to mix up our perceptions to appreciate the things around us.

Connecting with others and finding new angles can open up so many more opportunities and experiences. Whatever perception shapes your reality, make sure you enjoy the journey along the way. After all, you are the only person who has the power to control you. Making a choice, accepting consequences, and growing are all conscious acts that only you can do for yourself.

Every day presents an opportunity to choose how you perceive the world and respond to it. You are constantly shaping your reality through the lens of your perceptions and influencing those around you with the power you hold.

As we conclude, keep in mind that life is a journey, not a destination. If you've ever gone on vacation, you can surely recall all the planning that goes into it. You plan the main events, work out every detail, decide what time to wake up, determine when you'll leave, plan what you'll have for breakfast, and decide where you'll stop along the way.

Inevitably, something doesn't go quite according to plan during one of these trips. Often, these unexpected changes are the most memorable moments in the long run. Just as there is power in perception, there is also strength in the pause that allows us to reflect and enjoy conversations with others.

I remember a spring break trip my wife and I planned with our daughters. It was our first time taking a spring break vacation with them, something we had always wanted to do. My wife and I put a lot of effort into planning, though I must admit that she did the bulk of the organizing. We started by determining when our spring break would be and arranging time off from work. Then we looked for destinations. Considering how crowded it would be if we headed south, we decided to go north instead. Eventually, we chose the Mall of America as our destination.

As we prepared for the trip, we were excited but also a bit unsure, especially since we had never been there before and were uncertain about how things would turn out. Our kids weren't the best at shopping, particularly if it wasn't for them, and they were quite impulsive. So, we doubted that spending an entire day browsing and window shopping at the mall would be enjoyable for them.

However, we had planned several activities to keep them entertained, including taking them to a water park after a couple of days at the mall. We bought passes to one of their favorite water parks, which our kids had always loved and often begged us to go back to. Having visited a couple of times before, we knew they would enjoy it.

The next morning, we prepared them for the day ahead by telling them about our plans to go to the water park, promising a lot of fun. Shortly after settling in, the girls looked at each other, then turned to us and said, "Can we go back to the mall?" We exchanged glances, surprised but open to their request, and decided to head back to the mall instead. To our surprise, they had a blast shopping.

This experience reminded us that life is more like a journey than a series of planned events. Things don't always go as we expect, and we often learn valuable lessons along the way. When we remain open and self-aware, taking the time to pause and reflect, we can form deeper connections with others. You never know how these moments will enrich your life later.

The Road Ahead

Moving forward with purpose will cultivate an awareness of your perceptions and those of others. Such awareness brings power, which must be used responsibly. Understanding that your reality isn't *the* reality and that true power lies within will help you navigate any of life's detours. Successfully navigating the twists and turns ahead requires a balance of perception and power. Packing conscious self-awareness, an active search for other perspectives, and new definitions of power and control will prepare us for the journey. Being prepared keeps us open to learning and growth. Preparation helps keep us flexible and adaptable to new experiences.

Continued attention helps us stay on course. In our cars, we look out for road hazards, accidents, and stoplights. In life, we need to consistently look for new angles and opportunities. Self-reflection helps keep us focused on the road of life, continuously looking out for any twists and turns ahead. This is important because power is in the journey, not the destination. It takes time to build relationships, exert influence, and create change. Self-reflection keeps our perceptions and power in balance.

Your actions determine the impression you leave in the world, and they come from choice. All of this takes place inside and is not dependent on external forces. You can choose to get in the car and start your journey, but you can't choose if someone cuts you off in traffic. Your next choice will determine your influence and relationships with others. You can choose to respond with road rage, or you can maneuver defensively and go about your journey.

Your perception likely impacts your choice in this situation: do you perceive this person as simply rude, selfish, and in a hurry, or is it possible they are anxiously trying to reach a loved one who has just been taken to the hospital after having a heart attack? Taking a moment to pause and reflect will allow you to choose which perception guides your actions.

A Final Thought

As we reach the end of this journey into the power of perception, I hope the lessons shared inspire you to see the world a bit differently, embrace the power within, and practice responsible use of power to contribute to the greater good around you. Taking the time to look for new perspectives provides new possibilities and unlocks the power to make change through relationships and connections. Challenging our current views provides growth and balance, the tools to achieve the power for change.

I encourage you to embrace this mindset: be aware of yourself, have confidence, and take moments to reflect. Engage in conversations, build relationships, and remember that life is a journey filled with unexpected lessons if you're open to learning and growing.

As you move forward, remember that perception is not a fixed view; it is a dynamic, evolving force that shapes how we see and interact with the world. Power, when balanced with awareness and empathy, becomes a tool for growth, connection, and transformation.

Continue to reflect, stay curious, and use your perception and power to create a life that is both fulfilling and impactful. The path forward is yours to shape.

Thank you for reading. Your time is as valuable as your perceptions. Hopefully, this time has inspired you to pause and take in new sights and sounds. May this pause bring a world of new possibilities and grant you the power to create connection and change.

May your journey of perception and power continue to inspire and guide you, wherever it may take you, and may your actions inspire others.

THANK YOU FOR READING MY BOOK!

Just to say thanks for buying and reading my book, I would like to connect and offer you some free resources for your journey!

Scan the QR code:

I appreciate your interest in my book and value your feedback, as it helps me improve future versions. I would appreciate it if you could leave your invaluable review on Amazon.com with your feedback.

Thank you!

www.ingramcontent.com/pod-product-compliance
Lightning Source LLC
LaVergne TN
LVHW090518110826
845146LV00003B/906